NO MORE SECRETS

Malakh Zebulun

Publisher: Me and My Publishing

Photography: Good Knight Productions

ISBN: 978-0-9929449-0-2

WARNING:

This book is not a recommended read for young readers due to its graphic nature!

This book contains graphic accounts of violence involving sexual and physical abuse towards a child and adult. It is advised that you take great care of your emotional and mental health if you continue to precede reading.

At the back of this book Malakh Zebulun has added a few services that works directly with young people affected by domestic violence; or women ready to break their continuous negative cycles they find themselves in, in harmful relationships. Although Malakh herself has links with some of these organisations and companies, this book is independent from those services so you will need to ensure you research them properly yourselves.

If child abuse or domestic violence affects you, there are people and services out there able and willing to help. It starts with you taking a leap of faith and reaching out for help. You can either ask to be sign-posted by your general practitioner; at your local police station; your community support services or by contacting them discreetly by getting their numbers from a telephone directory or searching the internet for the information you need.

Stay safe and take care of you!

CONTENTS

Prologue

This story is about me, the author. I will take you on my journey and experiences of child abuse that went undetected by my large and very loving family. I expose my confrontation with bouts of mental anguish, an eating disorder, suicidal attempts, drug abuse and homelessness by the age of sixteen.

I reveal how my learnt experiences and feelings about myself led me to embrace negative and abusive relationships in my adult life. Alongside the effects of post-traumatic stress syndrome associated with abuse, I also embraced the experiences and emotions of abandonment.

Many victims and survivors of abuse live in silence; with many entangled feelings and an enormous shame for their plight, with deep-rooted anger and lack of self-love. I hid behind my professional career to silence my own vulnerabilities and shame until I was desperate enough to reach out for help at different times and until I gained the courage through exhaustion to begin to self heal.

I tell my story through my eyes as a child and then as an adult.

Why am I sharing my story and journey through child abuse and domestic violence?

I have spent decades of my life passionately dedicated to working with and helping young people and adults to develop their own skills, knowledge and even their confidence. This will hopefully assist them to overcome personal difficulties or challenges that they may confront across many aspects of their lives. Helping them to ultimately find the best solutions for their problems or concerns in order to move their lives forward and achieve their personal goals. Yet, I found myself secretly trying to handle my own real-life dramas that kept repeating itself in my own journey of life and would take me from one abusive or negative relationship to another.

I have spent many years accepting responsibility for what now happens in my life and working on my own self-worthiness, my confidence, my personal gratitude to past and future life encounters; and learning to release and forgive those who contributed to helping me reinforce the infliction of pain and hurt into my life; whether it was sexually, physically, emotionally, spiritually or mentally.

The journey of self-healing was long and hard but I have now broken and overcome the cycle that ultimately devalued my worth; feelings; emotions; lack of expectations for my own future; and the inability to reach out for help. I recognise I have now overcome the worst hurdles I am ever likely to experience where fear ruled me in my relationships or obstructed my inner-growth, personal joy and my deep rooted happiness because I refused to embrace the courage I needed and the responsibility to make it different.

I am now in a healthy and self-loving position in my own life that it has become a personal mission of mine to help and encourage as many people as I possibly can, whose lives are being affected by past hurts, to begin their new journey by reaching out for help and support. Most importantly, to begin their journey to self-healing so that they too will feel empowered to accept only the positive, nurturing and loving relationships into their lives.

I now believe it is possible and important to live a renewed, enriched and healthy life. I've learnt a life where we are in-tune with our own personal and spiritual purposes will bring about joy and happiness, as long as we can overcome the fear to accept and embrace such visions for our own lives.

I am blessed with a loving family. However like many families and communities alike, child abuse and domestic violence is not openly spoken about which can make the disclosure process for the victim a daunting and difficult task when trying to be heard or reach out. I hope my story will enable those affected and not affected alike, by the ills of child abuse or domestic violence to begin to understand the conditioning of fear and tolerance levels for victims of abuse who most often than not are unable to walk away from the danger they find themselves in at the earliest opportunity and how unconditional love and support from friends and family can make the ultimate difference when they become ready to embrace change.

Also I hope the reader can begin to gain an awareness, of how the mind-set and the pattern of behaviours which may be exhibited in secret by many abusers whose ultimate need will always be power, because of their own insecurities and will often deliberately manipulate and hide such behaviours from others.

My biggest hope is that anyone reading this book that has held on to their secrets relating to abuse, which was inflicted in their lives, finds the courage to release it from the depths of their spirit in the best way they can. Living with the pain and memories of past negative experiences can eat away at your soul. I pray you find the confidence to embrace life (as I have done and is possible) to live a purpose-filled and happy life without such secrets eating away at you like a disease. I want you to know, that you really are worthy and blessed. Best of all, if you're reading this......you've made it through already. Now its time to let go and live life!

Acknowledgements

I am so very blessed to be surrounded by so much unconditional love and support in my life.

Without this, life would have been unbearably painful. I love my mother and my stepdad with all my heart and it is their openhearted kindness and family orientated approach that attracts both family and friends into a fun-loving environment that is not easily forgettable.

My love for all my siblings, especially the heart-felt gratitude I feel towards my eldest sister Michelle, my 'almost twin' brother Roger and my cousin Ebony who have all been my confidant and rock during the hardest times of my life. To them, I thank them for always looking out for me and their nieces with a vengeance of love; and to my aunts, uncles, younger cousins, my sisters by choice; Carol Harroo and Rose Alexander along with my nephew Marlon who remains closely knitted into the values of family and each others lives, I thank you for sharing the importance of celebrating family.

Some of my oldest friendships goes back some thirty-six plus years with people I consider to be an extension to my family and through all my times of hardships and celebrations of joy they have been there and have always believed in me and held me in the highest regard. They have never doubted my potential to overcome and succeed. So to Tessa Simon, Deborah Millen, Susan Kearney, William Bryant, Tenny Thompson and Wendy King, Maxine Golden, I say thank you and I love you all dearly.

My gratitude and love can never forget the encouragement from dearest long-term friends like Kristine Wellington, Paul Vincent, Sandra Jarvis, Geraldine Nolan, Denice Houslin, Lorna Muhammad and some new ones too; Samantha Sutherland, Usha Oliver, Tia Tipton, and my church family.

To my children Theka and Eshe, you are the greatest gifts I have ever been blessed to receive in my life and I thank God for such treasures everyday of my life. When I needed more strength, faith, focus and love, God granted me you.

To my God-daughter Rowena you are so precious and dear to me and your beloved mother and my best friend Samantha Skinner who took my secrets to her early grave. I will love you forever and I still miss you intensely.

To a good man who always appreciates and celebrates me as I am, whether in business, social arenas or in a personal relationship, I thank my fiancé, Maurice Ellington for encouraging me to share my story with others, with the belief that I can help others to strengthen their hopes, faith and empower change by my stepping out. Thank you also for knowing I am worthy and deserving of greatness and love.

Above all, I thank God for His presence, patience, love, blessings and lessons in my life. I have never felt unloved by Him and I know He has brought me out from the wilderness when it was time and when He knew I was ready to receive a life filled with purpose. He lifts me up when I am weak and has carried me over many deep waters. God, I love and thank you for the gift of faith and choosing me to do your Will.

To those who have hurt me along the way, I FORGIVE YOU sincerely and thank you for helping to turn me into the emotionally intelligent and loving person I am today.

REVIEWS:

'This is a truly harrowing and honest account which, at times, was so upsetting it was difficult to keep reading.

Malakh Zebulun is incredibly brave and strong, not only for having endured all of these terrible things in her life, but also for having the courage to write her tale down and share it with the world.

This book is yet another reminder that we should and must be doing more to protect and identify those children and women who are being subjected to domestic violence and sexual abuse and that all communities in Britain need to be better educated to be able to spot the signs in friends and family members.

Malakh has chosen to use her terrible experiences to help others going through similar ordeals and for this she should be highly commended.'

~ **Emily Thornberry MP, Shadow Attorney General and MP for Islington South and Finsbury**

'Violence and abuse of women and children is a very hard topic to face for most, but it happens on a daily basis and is something that needs to be addressed. I commend and thank Malakh for sharing her story in this compelling book and hope her courage will inspire others to speak out and start their own healing processes'.

~ Baroness Sandip Verma

'I just roared through your book. Such a sincere outpouring, asking for nothing, giving all of you, touching me. Thank you for every word of it Malakh. I trust that some will be healed by reading it, some will be affronted, some awakened, some embarrassed and all will be privileged to share your Self unfolding. Thank you'

~ Joseph Seiler MCC, Author of Up From Paralysis

'Malakh has really opened up her heart in the book, baring her inner most secrets in her quest to help others. I take my hat off to her for her bravery and above all her ability to forgive. Malakh is an inspiration to others and I wish her every success as she goes on to help others overcome the long terms effect of abuse'

~ Vanessa Vallely CEO of We Are The City

'Malakh Zebulun has written a moving story that will touch your heart and soul. NO MORE SECRETS portrays a humanoid depiction of research and government statistics churned out so frequently that public interest has become slightly numbed to the heartbreaking fear that many children endure whilst subjected to ongoing incest/sexual abuse within the family unit.

No more secrets is a poignant read for professionals, parents and even culprits. Malakh Zebulun's gritty descriptions of her abuse enabled me – as a reader - to visualise the scenario and feel her childhood pain, humiliation and later, shame.

I applaud this lady's courage to share her unfortunate life-experience in such an open and humbling manner.

I would recommend NO MORE SECRETS to adults who have been subjected to child abuse and as adults, still living with their secret, afraid and ashamed to speak out against the perpetrator.

Another issue that Malakh Zebulun so eloquently described is the harsh discipline administered by some parents in the Caribbean communities. This harsh discipline disempowers a child, leaving many unable to approach their parents when they are being abused in this way. The interrupted innocence of a child has a long-term effect on the adult they become. The adult choices are usually bad choices based on the person's low self-esteem and self-hatred.

I thank Malakh Zebulun for sharing her story and writing her timely book which is a must read for all'.

~   Angela   Edmondson,   CEO   &   Founder   of DiversityInCare Ltd

Forward

Child abuse and domestic violence against women is a real scourge, which occurs all over the world. Its tentacles are capable of reaching women regardless of their age, colour, ethnicity, class, education, sexuality, disability, profession, lifestyle, religion, or bank balance. The statistics of its occurrence are as varied as they are astounding – depending on which academic, government, or charity/non-governmental organisation presents them. In the United Kingdom alone, it is said that at least 1 in 4 women will experience domestic violence in their lifetime. Some other countries do not bother to compile statistics.

The differences in geographical locations and their judicial systems notwithstanding, some features are constant. The shame, the isolation, frustration, and expectations of silence imposed on victims of domestic violence are almost generic. The human elements are not explored as deeply. Therefore, the statistics, where they exist, do not reveal the intensity of the pain suffered by victims of domestic violence. The statistics also do not disclose the depth of the character of the survivors. Or the hope they find, and cling to, in order to successfully make the transition from *victim* to *survivor*. But then, the statistics wouldn't. Statistics are about numbers.

The numbers of women who do exit abusive situations, and actually go on to live long, fulfilling lives are not as documented as the abusive situations themselves. And that is what *No More Secrets* is about. Ultimately, it is a celebration of hope.

The resilience of the human spirit is an incredible thing. Humans have proven over time, that the ability to bounce back from devastating circumstances is innate. As is the power to use seemingly ugly pasts as the raw material for beautiful, solid futures. We continue to prove that moving on is not a pipe dream, regardless of the particular circumstances. Our very existence is testament to our demonstration of 'moving on might be hard to do, but hard doesn't mean impossible'.

Living requires more than just being there. Moving from a plane of existing into the realm of living, takes courage. It takes courage to believe that there is more, that you deserve better than being trapped in an abusive situation, that you owe yourself more.

I was trapped in much a similar position, but courage, faith, determination and the love and support of people who care saw me through. Hence I love the way dear Malakh brings to light the trials, terrors and tremors of the past, and how she has decided not to allow her past to determine her future and to make a brave and courageous move to write this amazing book. It gives others help, support and hope for the future. A heart rending and moving book, it has touched and blessed my life. My prayer is that many thousands will read, relate and rise up and be called blessed.

Malakh found the much-needed courage to move past the horrors of a past, to a wonderful future of resilience, courage and success. I am confident that every reader who is currently in, or has gone through trials will glean the courage to truly live from the pages of *No More Secrets*.

Dare to dream. Dare to live. Dare to stand up and be counted as we did....

~ **Usha Oliver, CEO, Dare To Dream**

What is child sexual abuse?

'Child sexual abuse is when someone uses a child for his or her own sexual pleasure and gratification. An abuser may be a man or woman, or another child or adolescent. Both boys and girls can be abused, and sometimes from an early age.'

Protecting children from sexual abuse: A guide for parents and carers, NSPCC, 2008

'Sexual abuse of children is not a rare occurrence. It happens at all social levels, in all parts of the country, in all races and cultures. But despite increased public awareness, the true extent of child sexual abuse remains hidden. Conservative estimates suggest that one in ten children will experience some degree of sexual abuse – that's one million children.'

http://www.barnardos.org.uk/what_we_do/our_projects/sexual_abuse.htm

Chapter 1: Beverley

'Get to bed. I'm taking your sister and brother down to the launderette with me and I don't want to find you up when I return, if not there will be trouble Beverley,' penetrated my mother's voice as she walked out of the door of our snugly-fit first floor family flat. She pulled behind her, that old brown synthetic shopping trolley that had encountered and endured years of strain after bringing home our weekly shopping and transporting unbearable weights which would have benefited from being placed in a boot of a car, which we did not have. Today, that old trolley was packed full

15

with dirty linen. Outside the front door stood my eldest sister and my slightly younger-than-me brother, each holding black bin liners also filled with dirty washing. Both had a smug grin across their faces. Instantly, I could read their non-spoken dialogues. 'Ha! We're both going out with mum this time of night and you're not.'

Well at least I didn't have to carry any of those heavy loads; I tried to console myself with in retaliation of my thoughts. But really inside I felt like crying out 'how come he can go but I can't? He's younger than me' or 'how comes I'm the one who always gets left behind?' Better still, I wish I had rebelled and acclaimed, 'see they are your favourites'.

Being second eldest was no joke in my mind and world, when it came to family. Although to be honest it really didn't matter who or how many children came in between first girl and first boy or last child, often referred to as the baby of the lot. The rest were simply numerically numbered within this specially allocated ranking designed by adults. I had already learnt at the age of eight that it didn't matter what preferences, ideas, opinion, choices or reasons I had to something. If the eldest girl and boy or the baby of the lot said their piece it generally followed by my name being shouted out from any adjourning rooms; followed by 'behave you self.'

Forget coming back with 'but I didn't do nothing' as I constantly heard my reply before my words had even been spoken with the warning 'you hear me?'

On this occasion, I just stared back hard at my brother and sister and managed to conjure up my own smug facial expression with all my effort to prove I didn't care. But I did. The last words I heard my mother mutter again as she entered the lift was 'Beverley, don't let me find you still up, you hear or there will be trouble?'

That day when I closed that door, my life changed.

As I turned around the only corner in our hallway I immediately bumped into Terry whom I had only just a couple of minutes ago seen in the sitting room. He had been relaxing on the sofa with his feet up on the square pouffe watching the telly when I had walked past to follow mum to the front door, now he was standing there just staring back at me. 'Don't be giving me them looks' he ordered me. I felt puzzled and totally confused about what he was referring to. 'You heard your mother, behave yourself if not I'm going to beat you myself.' I immediately felt a sense of fear run through my bones. I had never heard Terry ever speak to any of us children like this. He always told mum in front of us that she had well behaved and lovely children. Now he was in front of me about to tell me off about something and immediately I knew whatever it was, I didn't do it.

'You think I don't see them looks you give me? Well I'm going to show you what happens to children who think they can look at adults like that and get away with it.'

'I didn't do anything' as soon as the words had left my mouth Terry grabbed my left ear lobe and started pinching it. The pain that engulfed me overtook my senses and my head immediately felt like it was overheating. 'Ouch, you're hurting me,' I cried and tears immediately began pouring from my eyes as my legs began to buckle and give way under the pain.

'I will make sure you know what happens to little girls who think they are too smart.'

The confusion was causing my mind to try and catch up. I didn't know what I had done that warranted my punishment. His pinching was hurting me more than a thousand times harder than the pinches mum ever gave me. The difference would be that she would have at least had given us a warning first that there would be trouble if we did not stop arguing amongst ourselves or if she thought one of us was not sharing with the others. But today, I really had no idea what it was that I had supposed to have done wrong.

'Stop the noise if not you will get beaten, here and now.' The threat silenced me immediately and reduced me to humming out a bass-like sound from behind my gritted teeth. With my obedience achieved, Terry released his grip on my ear and both my hands immediately flew up to comfort my stinging and throbbing lobe whilst my tears continued its flow into a running stream that I could feel landing on my nightclothes and bare feet.

Terry's hand slid behind the back of my neck and head. With that positioning, I felt his hand begin to restrict my head movements even further than when he was pulling on my ear lobes. This time my head was locked in the forward position and as much as I tried to move, my head, I could not turn to the left or the right in my attempt to release his grip. 'You're hurting me,' I tried pleading.

'I told you to stop the noise. You didn't hear?' He warned again. I began to notice his other hand moving towards my face but instead it landed on the buckle of his belt, which sat securely around his waist.

'Please don't beat me. I didn't do nothing' I desperately tried to defend myself from what I believed was the verdict of lashes as a punishment that would soon be meeting my skin.

Terry appeared to switch the tone of his voice with his next communication with me, as if trying to reassure me he said, 'I am not going to beat you'. I wiped away the tears as they were obstructing my vision as I kept a full watch on that hand. Terry continued to undo his buckle until both ends of the belt dropped open and hung from the tabs of his trousers. Trying to reassure me again he repeated, 'ok I am not going to beat you but if you hurt me I will knock your head off.' I looked up at him thinking what do you mean if I hurt you? 'Didn't I tell you not to look at me like that?' Immediately I dropped my face back down to the eye level of his belt. Terry had undone the button on his trousers and was now pulling down the zipper that began to expose his sky blue colour underpants. I had only ever seen my brother in underpants and somehow I immediately sensed I should not be looking. I tried turning my face away again but Terry's grip made it impossible to facilitate this movement as a response. Both my hands were still nursing and soothing the pain on the left side of my head when Terry began moving himself to position his back up against the wall which maneuvered me into a new standing position still connected by a neck hold. That made my right hand loose grip of my left ear and fall instead to rest on his arm that was holding my neck. I began to push against it to try and force Terry to release his grip but this still seemed an impossible task to accomplish and his grip tightened. Again he ordered a reminder, 'did I not warn you to behave yourself? Keep your little skinny ass still.' With that warning the back of my right arm returned to wiping away more tears.

After taking two or three long mopping up wipes on the sleeve of my nightclothes, I was confronted in full view of Terry's private parts, which was now sticking out of his underpants in an upright position. His private part was horrible. I had only seen my brother's when showering with him and my sister. But Terry had lots of hair on his and it was a frightening size and sight. Terry continued easing down both his underpants and trousers until they dropped to the shoes on his feet. Fear grew in my body. I tried to gather my next thought or fighting action in response to what I was seeing but within that frozen second Terry shoved his privates into my mouth and ordered me to suck. I began chocking and tried desperately to keep my mouth open and pull away. 'I said suck and if you hurt me, I will beat you stupid, you hear?' With those orders he raised his left hand above my head as if to indicate a slapping motion. I tried to gargle a plea but found it impossible to get a clear word out. 'Stop talking and suck. If you bite me

I'll knock your head off.' With that, Terry began moving his waist back and forth. As he did this, his privates moved with him and began almost leaving and re-entering my mouth. I began heaving and made a regurgitating sound as I felt his privates hit the back of my throat. 'You dare be sick on me and I will beat you for the nastiness. Now suck,' he continued to threaten.

As Terry picked up speed I began trying to do as he told me. My jaws began to ache within seconds of feeling his thing growing in my mouth. The pain on my ear began to transfer to my jaw as I concentrated on the task he had ordered. The only thought I could clearly pass through my mind was I wanted my mum. The thought only brought me more tears. Terry began making some weird sounds. It sounded like he was saying 'mmmmm.' After listening to that for some time he swapped that sound with words, 'faster' 'slower' 'easy.' Both of his hands at some point had moved to holding my head and maneuvering it with a push or pull whilst he orchestrated the movement along with the words he was saying and at the same time sliding his back up and down on the wall.

I had no sense of time. Everything felt like it slowed down and it felt like mum had been gone for ages. I needed her so much. I knew mum would help me and she would not let Terry do this to me ever again. She would be angry with him and she would kick him and beat him up for doing this to me. Terry pulled my head off of his privates and touched that ball thing covered by lots of loose skin and hair at the bottom of his privates and ordered me to 'put it into my mouth and suck'.

This was the first time I had the chance to look up at him without the restriction of that thing in my mouth. 'I don't want to' is all I could think of saying.

Terry's right hand returned to my left ear and he pinched it again for a second or two and then returned his hand back to that loose skin thing and moved it forward telling me to suck. His other hand guided my head forward towards that thing until it touched my nose. It was sweaty and smelt like wee-wee. 'Suck or your ear will fall off tonight.'

My tears became more vocal, 'I don't want' I didn't even get to finish the sentence before I felt a slap on the top of my head.

'Open ya mouth and suck it.' With that Terry pushed my head forward with his left hand still on my head and used his other hand again to pull that thing forward as well as use some of the finger tips from that hand to touch my face until he located my mouth and eased it open. 'Open wider' he ordered. I did and he popped it in saying, 'suck me good.'

It tasted sweaty and something like a plum moved inside of that loose skin. I could feel the hairs in my mouth tickling the back of my throat. It felt like some of the hairs we're stuck in between my teeth as my teeth moved round and round with the sucking motion I felt something like fine string pulling at my bottom teeth. I hated this. I hated him.

Some minutes later Terry had me move back to his privates. Whatever action he had me carry out was guided by his direct orders of instructions. With each instruction he seemed to make slight changes to the noises or sounds he was making. At times these sounds sounded as if I was hurting him but then he would say 'faster' or 'just like that.' After such a long time had passed by, Terry's body began to tremble whilst he was still occupying space in my aching jaw. Both of his hands were now placed on my head and I began to feel him forcing my head forward whilst he pushed his waist forward at the same time. 'Stop suck,' was his last order and immediately I could feel a pulse coming from his privates. In a few seconds the pulse rushed up the length of his privates and something exploded into my mouth. I felt sick and scared both at the same time. I felt like I was choking and immediately I felt a cough or a regurgitation brew itself up from inside my throat. Terry must have sense this too and he dragged my head away to break the connection from him. My mouth was full of this yucky stuff, which began falling to the floor. 'Swallow it,' Terry ordered. But my body kept regurgitating and I knew I wanted to be sick. I think he did too and he shouted at me, 'get to the toilet' and pushed me away from him to go into that direction.

I had changed overnight and a new and confused world full of internal fear and dread now shaped a new me. But this was only the start of what was to come and would alter the life choices I took for the next three decades.

I once used to look back on this day and say to myself 'why didn't my mum take me? It would never have happened. I would never have been hurt and the person I now feared most in the world would never have been able to do what they did. I hated him and because I hated him I hated her and I hated me. Those words would often rule my head like a ferocious viper eating away at my tender mind and heart. 'If only you had let me tell you on your arrival home everything could have been so different. Instead you lived up to your promise when you opened the front door nearly two hours later and saw me standing in the dark hallway and you beat me for being out of bed that night. My further wailing brought me more beats that night until my mind became numb, it simply shut down and I became obedient, tired and slept.

The child with no internal voice when it came to expressing their emotional distress had taken occupancy within this mind from that very day and that tender young age. Such early training enabled its right and acceptance to be there and succumb to a frigid state of fear and immobility during those times when I wished I could draw deep down inside me and fight back at all those people whom I knew by my inner spirit, were abusing me or my trust in times to come.

No one noticed the changes but they were there. They were certainly there, as clear as daylight, but no one notice them. Why? Because I had already been labeled as the different one, the handful, the emotional one, the keep quiet and keep still child. No one noticed the weight I was carrying on these small shoulders or the anguish and the hurt that oozed out. No one heard the cries of anguish, the tears of fear or the voice shouting out for help. Why? Because I was simply expected to keep quiet and keep still. I discovered a new world filled with anger, frustration and loneliness.

At eight years old my innocence had been invaded. I was only a child!

'For many reasons, children and young people often do not tell anyone about the abuse they are experiencing. This is a major cause of concern because it means that they continue to suffer in silence, which can have both short- and long-term impacts on their wellbeing.'

Debra Allnock (2010) Children and young people disclosing sexual abuse: An introduction to the research, NSPCC, London

Chapter 2:   Childs play

My mother's a fair skinned woman whose true beauty radiates off of her charismatic personality and the openhearted family welcoming she shares with so many people. Mum is a short and weighty set woman in statue but with an ability to project herself tall and fearsome with her short commands during my long years as a child. A woman of mighty strength, stamina and endurance who had the ability to relinquish her own rights for understanding even her own emotions and sometimes I thought, the feelings of her own children. I wondered if this was because she too faced loneliness, isolation, hurt, abuse and abandonment of a different kind during her marriage to my dad and then as a single mother to four children.

Mum has always been a hardworking and giving woman. I remember mum holding down 3 jobs. Starting her day leaving the house around dawn to head off to her first job as an auxiliary nurse at Chelsea and Westminster Hospital; then by afternoon she was off to do the first of her private cleaning jobs for whom I believed on about the two occasions I remember mum having taken me along with her that the family's house where she cleaned must have been for a rich family, as their tastes of furnishings and crockery always seemed delicate and fragile. Then mum would be on to the next cleaning job in the evening. Somewhere along my childhood journey mum also became a bus conductor and her hours still appeared to be long and hard; rounding off her monotonous day by arriving home in the evening to put food in the mouths of her children. As I look back now, I can see and feel her struggles to get through it all on her own and no doubt praying for a better hand in life to be served to her. My mother probably dragged her tired self out of the bed and house in the morning and dragged it back home to bed again.

Mum comes from a large family whose roots hold strongly back in Barbados, an island I've known all my life but had never visited during my childhood. Our household and extended family up until that point was the Caribbean whether we were at home in South London or travelled over the Thames from Putney Bridge towards Fulham where our Gran and Granddad lived. The rest of the Caribbean could be discovered when we attended regular family or friends gatherings or went on seaside excursions by coach with the Bajan, Jamaican, Trinidadian or Grenadian households.

It was always expected to be the same bubbly household when we arrived along with the aunts, uncles, cousins and what seemed like the whole of London Transport ticket collectors or bus drivers whom had all met each other when they travelled over from the Caribbean to England in the fifties to early sixties on the large ships that brought them. Over the decades, their friendships were simply just an extension of my family. So like all my brothers and sisters, we just referred to everyone as aunty and uncle or what sounded like a more endearing term like Mrs. Henry or Mr. Pickering but never on first name basis.

These visits were generally never boring ones. Just about every household had at least two to four children also living in this Caribbean utopia. Each household also had carvings and embroidery wall hangings depicting the island of origin to which the premises belonged. Each had its middle of the room coffee table made of wood, glass or marble, which matched the free standing wall cabinet found in the centre piece of a room. If the room was generally a small one, then the free standing wall cabinet would still take centre place from the corner wall that could always be seen on entering that room. Each cabinet was host to an array of china ornaments, fancy glasses, sporting medals, old photographs and of course the dominoes set and several packs of playing cards. These tended to arrive onto coffee tables or dining tables, which were dressed first with a special cloth or plywood to avoid it being scratched. Most households stored these behind a sofa or somewhere out of sight until they were needed to host the community board games again.

There was never an individual leader in these adult activities as it always appeared to be dominated by every single adult who played. Each adult; added their own unique and overbearing character to the pot which would not be for the meek and mild partaker. It was evenings like this that the Caribbean felt even hotter. The heat from the sheer numbers of people packed into one household recreated the sunrays and heat across the air that was now available for breathing. Conversations were always loud and comical but never of any serious intellect. Simply fun and laughter always filled the air like families playing on the sea banks splashing back and forth at each other with banter. There was always so much food and alcoholic drinks. This of course was simply the cookout all Caribbean people did regardless of which island they belonged.

These were indeed fun times. A time when we as children could all stay up and out as long as we were visiting friends or family or they were visiting my grandparent's house. A time when all the children present could and would be disciplined as a group if one child found the other children a bit overbearing or if one child exercised their attempt to get the others in trouble then all of the children would speak up to the adult disciplining the accused child rushing in with their version to tell what actually happened and the accused child could easily be found not guilty and their voices heard. This was the best jury to have in your case. Your peers in these groups all came from different environments with similar backgrounds and chemistry; who could come to the same verdict if one child was acting unfairly. This group broke down the inconsistencies often found in the individual households simply because the voice of the innocent one tended to sound louder and clearer when a multitude of children were addressing an adult. I guess it generated the opportunity to clear your name and have the situation resolved within seconds as there was a more pressing need for the adults to get back on with their slamming down of dominoes and cussing out the others with their banter for the weaknesses identified in their opponent's current game.

As brilliant and fair as these evenings seemed, there were occasions when we knew that the looks we got from our parents dug deep into our little souls. We knew this would not be the last we would hear about a behaviour they felt was unruly or embarrassing to them. This indicated the preparation of the fear that was to come when that child got home. The other children always knew the signs of what was to come too. Their own home life when it came to Caribbean discipline appeared from these hard glares to be no different really than ours and I also believed they'd be getting beats too when they got home. Whether they did or not, I really never knew the extent of their plight and they never knew mine.

As difficult and emotionally challenging some of my young life felt, I absolutely loved being with my extended family that we would spend just about every weekend and half term with. Even if we had a half-day at school my brother, sisters and I would easily pine and persuade mum to let us all walk the two miles over to our Grandparents house. We knew once we arrived we would always receive an excited warm welcome from the children who lived on the two housing estates that faced opposite to our Grandparents house.

One of my uncle's sons Anthony lived with his mother just up the road from our grandparent's house. Anthony sometimes came over to visit when he knew we had arrived. He was somewhere between two or four years older than me and definitely the loudest and most boisterous out of the dozens of children gathered together. He often took most of the telling off because his clumsiness tended to result in him damaging something. He would either get excited and take his unbalanced and oversized body and leap onto something without judging the implications of his planned mission and break it. His favourite pass time was to see how many stairs he could leap down. We all did this, and would land as quietly as we could on the ground floor landing. Sometimes we would achieve five steps, sometimes six or sometimes seven, but often more than that we knew we would be heard and told off for jumping down the stairs. Anthony would achieve being told off even if he jumped three. His body shape did not allow gravity to place him gently on the ground floor. He always sounded like someone fell down twenty flights of stairs and ended at the bottom in need of the medics. Whenever Anthony took part in the game, it was brought to an end before we all took our turn.

I liked Anthony's mum. She seemed to like asking me how I was and what I was up to when she came over to our grandparent's house. This always seemed more apparent on a day when we were not allowed out to play with the stream of friends who crossed over the road from the housing estates and rang the doorbell from midday to dusk. On some of those days she would ask me if I wanted to come around to their house to play with Anthony and on a few occasions asked if I wanted to stay over. I would always say yes if I knew there was no chance we'd be allowed outside to play.

On the last occasion I can recall in my memory, Anthony's mum came over and I did leave with her. Anthony's room was full of Tonker Toys, which were these big trucks that we could load up lots of toy soldiers and Lego figures into its tip. Anthony also had lots of board games and an array of different sized footballs. Most of the balls appeared to be either soft or flat. Looking at them I remember always thinking to myself 'you sat on that didn't you?' I could never understand why he had to sit on everything he had. Was he testing the equipment or was he testing his strength? But whatever it was, it was never a surprise to see his possessions broken and destroyed.

After playing with the toys for a short while boredom seemed to have set in so Anthony asked if I wanted to play a mummy and daddy game. I enjoyed playing this with my sisters but often never got to be the mummy as my eldest sister always took that role. I was often the eldest child or the baby who wasn't allowed to talk that much. And when we played doctors and nurses I was always the nurse as my sister would always have the leading role as the doctor who gave the nurse orders when making that all important diagnosis on our younger brother or sister who were our guinea pig patients.

I remember thinking; at least with Anthony I will get the role as the mummy and won't have to complain about the other roles being dished out, as there was no one to dish them out to. So I accepted my role. Anthony decided that as the mummy I should dress up like one so he left the room and returned with his mother's red beaded clip on earrings for my starring role. I immediately declined the prop saying 'I'm going to get into trouble if aunt see me with them on'

'No you won't' Anthony persuaded 'mum doesn't wear them and I will say I got them and made you wear them' with that assurance making me feel even more comfortable; I accepted my prop and my role began.

For the first fifteen or so minutes I had to pretend I was making breakfast for my pretend husband and make his pretend packed lunch for his pretend work. He was a stern husband barking out all the orders and disapprovals about what was missing from the pretend dining table as he sat on the floor with his legs out straight mainly because he couldn't cross his chubby legs. He then got up from sitting on the floor and off to his pretend job he went whilst I cleared away the pretend breakfast, and then pretended to vacuum the floor while pretending to whistle. Then my pretend husband would return from his pretend work by knocking at the bedroom door. I opened the door to be greeted with 'where's my dinner, I'm hungry' and off I went to get the pretend food as he sat plonked down hard on to the floor with legs straight out again at the pretend table awaiting to be fed again.

'Let's play real mummy and daddy' Anthony suggested.

'I am' I declared in defense. Thinking that this greedy pretend daddy was now critically refuting my first proper chance I had to play the starring role.

'Don't you know how to play real mum and dad games' questioned Anthony. 'We have to pretend to make babies so then I will be a real daddy and you will be a real mummy.' Anthony could tell by my questioning squint that I did not know what he was on about. So he became the director of this new script and I followed the instructions so that I could learn my part.

'Lay down on the bed like you're going to sleep. Move over to the wall then I can fit in on this end and won't fall off the bed' Anthony ordered.

I got on top of his single bed and lay facing the wall. 'Ouch these earnings are hurting my ear when I lay down.'

'Give them to me' Anthony took the earnings and left the room to return them to wherever he found them and came back in to the room a few seconds later ordering me about with 'come on, lay down' as he closed the door.

'Alright!' He sounded like my eldest sister whenever I played with her she always told me what to do. I laid down and got myself as comfortable as I could then Anthony joined me lying beside me. As soon as he sat on the bed I felt gravity move me and I rolled away from the wall, as his side of the bed seemed to sink with his weight.

'Move over a bit' he said oblivious that he had caused me to roll. I shuffled over a bit which felt like climbing a mattress hill, but my body could not fight the gravity the more he moved and took more portions of the bed with his body the harder it was to keep my body from rolling. Finally he was fully on the bed. 'Ok this is what my mum and dad does, I've seen them. Lay on your back not facing the wall.' With that I maneuvered onto my back but with him lying next to me on the single bed I felt like my body was suctioned between the wall from shoulder to shoulder and unable to move. 'I have to lie on top of you but I won't squash you.'

'No way you're going to flatten me' I declared trying to get up and out of the game. I had seen Anthony sit on many of his victims which always seemed to bring him a sense of laughter as he watched them wiggle and unable to shift the weight from above them.

'No I won't, I told you I'm going to show you how to play real mummy and daddies.' As he spoke he rolled over and was now etched above me holding up his own weight by balancing with a bit of a tremble on one of his forearms and elbow. I felt his other hand slip underneath him and he appeared to be adjusting his shorts. 'You have to keep still though, if not it's not going to work.' Again his hand seemed to be fidgeting with his clothing until I felt something warm and a bit wet touching against the inside of my legs.

'What's that?' I couldn't quite make it out

'You'll see in a second, just keep still' He demanded, as he appeared to be concentrating hard on what he was doing above me. 'You have to put your legs on the outside not the inside of my legs' as I began to readjust my legs Anthony summoned his next instruction, 'Spread your legs open a bit more' He probably could sense my next why question so he responded quickly by saying 'you won't feel squashed then.' That sounded like the most sensible thing he had said at that moment as I felt like every last bit of breath had been squashed out of my body. So I obey and moved my legs and placed them on the outside of his. As soon as I had moved I felt my panties move to one side and some hard, long-like-finger-thing touch my private part and try to force it against me. I screamed thinking he put something in my wee hole and he cup his hand over my mouth as he moved his body up and down on me.

With Anthony cupping his hand over my mouth I felt glued to the bed and unable to turn to the left or right and did not have the strength to push his big fat weight from off of my tiny frame. Just then the door to his bedroom flew open and aunt; his mum stepped in. She grabbed his clothes on his back and almost swung him to the floor where I heard that all familiar thud on the floor, of Anthony landing as he always did; whilst at the same time aunt was shouting his name at the top of her voice. She then pulled me by the arm and stood me up and walked me straight out of the bedroom and closed the door behind her. Standing there in the passage aunt turned me to face her by directing her hand movement still attached to my arm to have me facing her. I thought she was about to shout at me and as she looked at me and spoke she instructed me in a quietly spoken voice and said 'go into my bedroom and I will be there to see you in minute.' Without a good bye she turned and walked back into Anthony's bedroom and closed the door. Immediately I could hear aunt shouting hard at him and then I heard what I knew sounded like slaps meeting his skin. These sounded both hollow and hard and were matched with his screams until I could hear him sobbing like a baby.

I waited in aunt's room frightened that I too was in trouble and was about to get my share of the beats for something I did not understand. After all, this was Anthony's idea of a game, not mine. Around the outside part of my privates and top part of my leg where my panty line ended, felt a little sore and when I looked at my legs I could see big red marks from where he had squashed and grazed me. I stood there in the middle of the bedroom until aunt arrived. This time her voice was gently and she sat on the end of her bed and pulled me nearer to her and then lifted me up onto her lap as she said 'you are not to speak about this again and you must never tell your mother what Anthony just did. Do you hear me?'

'Yes aunty!'

I wasn't even sure at that stage what Anthony had done. But I knew after her words were spoken that he wasn't allowed to do it. She hugged me for what felt like two seconds and then told me to go get ready for dinner and I did. That night she put me to sleep in her room which I had never done before and she took me back to our grandparents house earlier than I recall her ever doing before when we woke the next morning.

I must have been around nine years old.

Crime statistics on sex offences

17,727 sexual crimes against children under 16 were recorded in England and Wales in 2010/11.

32% of all sexual crimes (54,982 sexual crimes in total) recorded in England and Wales in 2010/11 were sexual crimes against children under 16.

Chaplin, Rupert, Faltley, John and Smith, Kevin (eds.) (2011) Table 2.04. In: Crime in England and Wales 2010/11: findings from the British Crime Survey and police recorded crime (PDF). London: National Statistics. p.43.

Victims

Most of the victims of children and young people who display sexually harmful behaviour are siblings, extended family members, friends or neighbours (Awad and Saunders, 1989; 1991). Foster and step-siblings and those in care settings are particularly vulnerable. Some of those who display inappropriate or sexually abusive behaviour abuse either boys or girls, while others abuse both groups (Epps, 1999). The age of victims ranges from less than two years to adult.

Elizabeth Lovell (2002), Children and young people who display sexually harmful behaviour, NSPCC, London

Chapter 3: Cycle of abuse

Life at home was still an uncomfortable place to be when mum's boyfriend was around or stayed over. He was a muscled man who often walked around the flat with his shirt off his back or was always laying in bed. Whenever Terry came things changed. There were some things we all had to learn and took some time learning it. It was only when Terry was around we would discover and remember mum even had a lock on her bedroom door as this was the only time it was ever in use. So it became that whenever we arrived at mum's bedroom door on a Saturday morning, my siblings and I would not be able to gain entry. Soon we became accustomed to automatically knocking the door and waiting for the bolt to be released before we could do our usual routine of snuggling up next to mum in her bed and watch some Saturday morning telly before being sent to brush our teeth, eat our cereal or take our showers and get dressed.

I hated Terry. He still made me do horrible things to him even though mum never again left me in the house with him. Mum seemed to always ask me to go make him a cup of tea and I had grown to hate this man so much that I used to accidently-on-purpose make my saliva dribble into the cup whilst I was making his tea knowing that in the next few minutes he would be drinking it. I had even greater pleasure watching him drink it and not knowing how much hate was inside that cup.

There were plenty of times he would remain in the bed as my mother got up to fix up a cooked breakfast and return to the room with a food tower portion for this man. During my mother's trips to the kitchen I would fear my name being called by Terry, as I would have to go. Sometimes I would avoid going on the first call but after the second call my mum would call my name from where she was in the kitchen and shout to me 'Can't you hear your name being called' This was never really a question but a warning statement letting me know not to let her hear my name get called a second time and I don't reach the caller.

I would stand in the doorway of the bedroom and Terry would always use his index finger in a beckoning notion to indicate I needed to move closer and closer to him until I stood at the side of the bed to where he laid. Then he would throw back the covers and force my head down on to his privates whilst raising the other hand above my head in a slap motion threatening to hit me if I made any noise. I hated this man so much.

On just about every occasion I heaved and choked. My brain and mouth could not keep up with his movements. I just knew I hated him so much and wish he were dead so he wouldn't have to come back again. I couldn't understand how mum never caught him. But I also learnt how sneaky and sinister he was and like some beast would wait around and when the time was perfect would catch his prey.

After each abuse, he was always joyful and I always hated on him. He would compliment me as a really good girl and when mum noticed I would snub him would always ask me why I have to be so damn rude to him. The man was a pig. But there was no one to tell. All my extended family seemed to like him too. So whenever I heard good things said about him. I hated them too. I promised myself that when I was sixteen I would leave this place and no one could make me stay a day longer. Unless of course he dropped dead before that.

My grandparent's house became my sanctuary. My haven. Even though the house was filled to the brim with so many individuals to plan sleeping arrangements for when it came to night times; no two nights were ever the same depending on who was staying over. Aunt Carleen and uncle Royston also lived in the house. Then there would be my mum and her four children visiting, along with my cousin Neville and Patricia who was aunt Carleen's friend who stayed over all the time and any foster children my grandparents had looking after.

Mary George was one of those foster children who had arrived one night with her social worker and stayed for somewhere between six months and the year before being moved on to be placed with the next set of foster carers. She was already nearly sixteen years old and was by far the oldest out of all the children in the house. She was also another bossy boots but this time she spoke up to adults and said things we would never dream of, whenever the mood took her.

She slept in my auntie's room in the fold up single bed in one corner of the room whenever we visited, whilst my aunt slept in her double bed. The family decided as I had the smallest physique amongst the children it was more suitable for me to lay down next to Margaret when it came to sleeping times. The first night I slept next to her I felt her throw her arm over my body in a hug. This always reminded me of sleeping next to my sisters especially during the cold nights as we used the hugs or lying back to back as a way to keep ourselves warm until we fell asleep.

On a few earlier occasions Margaret gently stroked my arm which always felt soothing and often made me fall straight off to sleep as I laid tucked up on my side, flat up against the wall so that she'd also be able to fit on to this tiny bed without being bumped off the end by some sudden move I might make in my fidgeting or tossing during my sleep.

One night as I lay sleeping next to Margaret, I was slightly awoken by a warm sensation I felt somewhere mid way between my belly and my legs. I remember grumbling a little in my sleep as I felt this gently disturbance of something coercing my legs apart from each other. My eyes we still locked in sleep as my body twitched in its own little fight. As I struggled to awake myself I could not work out if I was in a dream and spent a few moments hanging on in the dream. I then heard something groan from inside

---

37

the sheets near the bottom of the bed. Immediately my eyes became wide open and I noticed something in a shadow form. It was a fuzzy ball liked shape, bobbing up and down under the sheets. I followed the outline of the shape and realised it was attached to a body and legs appearing out at the end of the sheets and was kneeling on to the floor from the side of the bed. I realised someone in this dark room was making some wet and warm feeling happen on my body. Immediately for a few seconds I froze. Who was this? This sensation was new and actually felt nice at the same time as fear began growing from my pounding heart. 'Please God help me,' was all I could think.

I jerked my body, as a motion to get this thing off me, whilst I began to push my hand on what I now knew was a head underneath the sheet. Immediately Margaret sat up with her mouth wet and one of her hands were down her panty. Then, whilst she was still on her knees, I thought she was going to be sick as her body gave this heaving or regurgitating motion as she fell head forward on to the bed breathing erratically, sweating and gritting her teeth. After about ten seconds of sinking her head, face down into the sheets from her sitting position on the floor. Margaret turned her head to face me and said, 'say a word to anyone and I will deny it and I promise you I will beat you up.'

This happened every time thereafter when I was placed to sleep next to Margaret. Even if I objected and said she slept badly, this was ignored by the adults; especially my mum who would simply tell me to go to bed and behave myself. The only nights I ever had any grace from Margaret's assaults on me was when my aunty Carleen decided she was going to her bed early; and then and only then did Margaret seemed to leave me alone on those nights. As quick as she had come, she was moved on without even a good bye one day.

Until this day, I have never forgotten her name although the features of the face of this young black girl with thick natural hair; has faded from my memory. I remember wondering if other children had ever been inflicted by her abuse and if the reason she had been taken in to care was because someone had abused her. All I knew is, if she had been abused, I would never understand why she would inflict others as she had done me. From that very young age, I was already absolutely convinced I would never-ever ever-ever do this to any other human being and would never-ever ever-ever hurt a child deliberately in this or anyway other way.

Again I was faced with not telling a soul about what was happening. All these people were getting away with doing these things to me and I was never allowed to tell because of the threats that they made to me. By now I started to believe I was brought into this world for this sole purpose. I had no idea what to do or how to handle it. So instead I simply lived up to labels that my family kept adding to my list of names like, the emotional one or the black sheep. It had now been declared by most members of the family, that I was probably like this because I missed my dad. He had now been labeled as a wicked man after mum left him with her children in hand and never returned to our family home in Aylesbury again. My gran often made negative comments about my dad and constantly kept feeding me and my brother and sisters stories about the wickedness of this man which constantly had my mum fearing for her life and for her children until she had arrived safely back at our grandparents home when I had just turned five years old.

However I was now hitting my eleventh birthday and knew that my emotions were not really related to missing my dad, but I went along with their theory, anyway.

Most serious sexual offences accounted for 82 per cent of total sexual offences and one percent of all police recorded crime in 2010/11. There were 45,326 most serious sexual offences recorded in 2010/11, a four per cent increase compared with the 43,439 recorded in 2009/10 These offences include rape, sexual assault, and sexual activity with children.

• Police recorded rapes of a female increased by five per cent to 14,624 offences and sexual assaults on a female increased by four per cent to 20,659 offences.
• Rapes of a male increased by 12 per cent to 1,310 offences and sexual assaults on a male increased by seven per cent to 2,412 offences.

Chaplin, Rupert, Faltley, John and Smith, Kevin (eds.) (2011) Table 2.04. In: Crime in England and Wales 2010/11: findings from the British Crime Survey and police recorded crime (PDF). London: National Statistics. p.62

Chapter 4:   Rape by any other name

Anthony's brother Neville had lived at our grandparent's house for a few months after his dad sent for just him to return to England having migrated to Jamaica with his brother, sister and his mum who was now my uncle's ex-wife. Anthony and Neville had different mothers. Neville was then about sixteen years old. He was one of the eldest of all the grandchildren so fell into the category of being a favourite quite easily by my grandmother who simply adored him. Maybe that was because he was the child of her own eldest and first-born son.

Neville was nothing like Anthony. Neville was handsome, tall and was a pleasure to be amongst. He was fond of all his cousins and had something in common with my sister. They both shared the same birthday, just three years apart.

Not long after Neville's arrival to England he moved into our home and was enrolled into the same school that I went to with my eldest sister and brother. My youngest sister was still in primary school and the new baby of the lot who was eleven years my junior attended nursery school which now brought my mum's child bearing blessings, to five.

It was great having my cousin live with us and going to the same school. Just about every girl who met him fell head over heels and revealed their lustful intentions and silly notions when he came into their presence or they mentioned his name. In school I was often sent with messages by the same friends to pass on to him either immediately by standing at the bottom of the sixth form block until someone who recognised me as Neville's cousin would go and fetch him for me so that I could pass on the message or I was questioned about what he said when I returned to school the next day. Most times he laughed it off but later I would always hear he had had some fling with those whom I had carried these messages for.

Neville appeared to have the same affect on many of the girls whom lived in the flats opposite our grandmother's house. They couldn't help but fall for his smooth slick persona. He was charismatic, gently and attentive. No one ever seemed to have a bad word to say against him.

If I ever felt low he always stepped in and made me smile simply by asking me to smile. He never got told off because there was never a reason spoken or found for anyone to tell him off for. He was also my knight in shining armour and often gently stepped in when I was being chastised for something and would come to my defence. Before I knew it, I was feeling less of a target from the accusations from my siblings than I had been in the past. I simply loved him just for that.

Christmas was indeed a special occasion with our large and extended family. I can never recall us staying at our home in Putney as my brothers, sisters; cousin and I would simply have rebelled and complained if we had. These were always enjoyed at our grandparent's house. Our massive Christmas tree was always a real tree that granddad would bring into the house to our delight. The tree with its fairy on top always touched the ceiling and had an array of decoration and lights on it that I have not seen replicated on any other tree in any other house, to this day. The presents were always plentiful. Those coloured wrapped parcels where piled high under the tree and seeped out to about a quarter of the through-lounge. Looking back now, it seems amazing that there were so many as most of the gifts given to my mum were to be shared amongst all of her children. I guess it shows how many people also stayed or would be coming to that house.

Christmas was definitely a time for family. Both children and adults spent tons of time playing the new and old board games, creating teams and projecting tons of laughter. I used to love charades. There was always one person every year who would make the naming that book, film, TV programme or play even harder than it needed to be, simply because they couldn't spell and tried to describe the name of their mime with either too many or too little syllables. Each year just before starting this game again everyone would begin the journey of reminiscing about who messed up the year before and then proceed through the years and name and shame. This always helped to start this game in laughter and exposed that child or adult under a spotlight as if to predict they would be silly enough to make themselves the target for that year's game. I loved spending time with my family. Our family was certainly large and Christmas was always focused on the children and the family. To be honest, the only thing slightly different at Christmas was the door bell wouldn't be ringing out its tune continuously all day by our endless streams of friends asking for us to come out to play. No one left the house and we would all eat together instead of in cluster groups. Today was stay in and do indoor things with the family, which brought together my brothers, sisters, mum, cousins, aunties, uncles and grandparents. There must have been almost twenty of us.

We were used to noise levels and the 'nowhere to go' in this three bedroom house for any peace and quiet. Wanting to be on your own was almost frowned upon when you were a child and you would be told to go back in the room with the rest of the children. If you sat on the stairs too long you were told to stop blocking up the stairs and if we were seen in the passage lingering around too long, one of the adults would walk past on their way into the through-lounge or heading in the other direction to the dining room and kitchen and asked you, 'why you out here?' followed by 'go-long inside the room.'

Sleeping arrangements during Christmas time was a bit more chaotic. The floor spaces had to be allocated out too. If you had spent more than two or three nights as a child sleeping on the make shift bed on the floor then you were more likely to be able to get a fairer hearing for being nominated for one of the sofa's or armchairs and use the 'it's not fair card' against the child hogging their bed like gold dust.

This one particular Christmas, it would have been my second night allocated to the bed space made up on the floor in the through-lounge. So I took my second night as humbly as I could, knowing I wasn't going to be allowed to move just yet. Anyway it was already late hours into the morning, which was never a surprise to be up so late when

---

43

we were at our Grandparents house. Mum slept letting out some deep snores on the sofa with my brother Raymond, the baby of the lot, and the upstairs three bedrooms were already taken. Some of the men in the family and some family friends were still up and playing their game of dominoes or cards which slowly moved itself to continue in the kitchen where the only ones they might disturb with their slamming on the table was Kitty or Lucky, the cats and Curly the dog.

I had no knowledge when I fell off to sleep as to who ended up sharing my floor space and covers with me. Somewhere between that deep sleep-zone I had entered, I was awoken. Someone lying behind me had alarmed my body and proceeded to frighten my mind and spirit. The position of their hand and the covers still over my shoulders told me they were inside the bed and lying down very closely next to me. I felt a hand stoke itself across the bare flesh of my bottom. Immediately I realised my panties had been arched down and were now sitting below my bottom and at the top of my thighs. Someone had moved them and that someone was now touching me. I was so frightened I couldn't move and definitely feared turning around. I was physically paralyzed. In this dread I froze still with only my thoughts moving and my heart racing. 'Please God make them go away. Make them stop, please God help me.' These pray thoughts brought streams of tears in a continuous flow from my eyes as I lay on my side. I could feel the pillow case becoming wet as I lay there in the dark trying to look around with just my eyes without making my head move. I opened my mouth to call my mum when I spotted her asleep on the sofa. But as much as I wanted her and needed her right now, no word would depart from my lips. I felt so petrified that I could feel my body beginning to shiver from inside with fear. I could literally feel it shaking as the fear intensified. My mind was telling me to pretend I'm sleeping maybe they will leave me alone. 'Please God don't let them do this. Someone help me please.' Still I could not speak.

The hand began moving and was now heading over my leg towards my private parts. They had to feel me shaking. There was no way they couldn't. I had to do something and I had to do it now. So to indicate I was still asleep, I pretended to give a disturbance groan and make my body toss and turn as if to warn them away from waking me up. So I did. I gave a short groan and started to roll myself over onto my tummy so to stop their hand from reaching and touching my privates. Before my body managed to complete the roll and my stomach touch the floor, the person owning that hand; sunk themselves even closer to me. I could feel their breathing on my neck and cheek. They began kissing my shoulder and at this same time that hand continued its journey attempting to tuck itself under my stomach instead. In one quick and firm movement, which I so did not expect this hand rolled me back to the position I had just come from. 'Help me someone, help me, please someone,' still my mind did all the shouting and not a sound fell beyond my lips.

The person placed themselves up tight against my back. I could feel their thing. They started to move it around my bottom. It was wet, hard and warm. 'Help me someone. Mum wake up, please mum I need you.' From the body scent of the person I guessed it was Neville. He began to perspire as he tried to position his thing where my thighs finished and my bottom began. As I lay there I had flash back about Anthony his brother some five and a half years earlier.

I felt the same hand turn itself to one of my bum cheeks and it felt like they were using it to anchor open my legs by separating my bum cheeks to open it up. They made one last wiggle and then I felt this excruciating pain as they entered me. No one had ever done this before. Not even Terry, Anthony or Mary George. Even though Anthony had tried, I realised his mum had actually saved me from this next bit.

I'm not sure how long he carried on for. To me it was eternal. I still tried my best to pretend I was sleeping but my breathing and the slight noises it made me project had changed to a faster speed. I heard myself slip out the odd groans as the pain intensified. He was kissing my neck as he carried on and I wasn't sure if he heard them or not. 'Why does the world hate me' is all I could conquer up in my mind as I laid there with tears still continuously streaming down my fake sleeping squinted face. 'Well I definitely hated the world too' is all I could answer that question back in my mind.

As much as I did not want this, my body began to feel different as he moved that hand again back over my leg to attack me from the front of my privates at the same time. Even under all this fear there was a sensation that was arousing through my body as he stroked me with that hand over my privates. I had never experience what he was doing and never experienced this sensation either. My body was acting like it liked it. Whilst I lay there frightened, and hating my cousin for doing this to me.

I heard him make some groan sound in the back of his throat whilst he stiffened up his body. As he did that his thing inside seemed to explode and I could feel his body shaking like it was in spasms. He stopped touching me and removed himself from invading me, to flop over on to his back. He was breathing fast. I kept as still as I could and refused to let myself move an inch. 'You bastard, I hate you, I hate you, I hate you, and I hate you' more of the same thoughts keep generating through my mind and still I couldn't say anything.

About three or four minutes later I could hear Neville snoring lightly.

I was just fourteen and a half years old when I was raped and I told know one.

Symptoms of depression

Listed below are the symptoms of depression as described by the International Classification of Diseases (ICD 10), which is the criteria that can be used to diagnose mental health problems. Not everyone who is depressed will experience every symptom. Some people experience a few symptoms, some experience many. Severity of symptoms varies between individuals and also varies over time.

➢ Low mood and feeling sad
➢ reduction of energy and decrease in activity
➢ loss of interest and enjoyment in pleasurable activities
➢ loss of concentration
➢ tiredness after little activity
➢ sleeping and eating less (although sometimes this can increase)
➢ loss of self-esteem and self-confidence
➢ guilt or worthlessness
➢ loss of sex drive
➢ suicidal thoughts and acts

What are the different types of depression?

Depression can come in different forms and in different degrees. For the purpose of management and treatment the most common types of depression are often referred to as the following3.

Mild depression

Two or three of the above symptoms are usually present. The patient is usually distressed by these but will probably be able to continue with most activities.

Moderate depression

Four or more of the above symptoms are usually present and the patient is likely to have great difficulty in continuing with ordinary activities.

Severe depressive episode

An episode of depression in which several of the above symptoms are marked and distressing. Suicidal thoughts and acts are common and the person may need to go into hospital.

Depression Fact Sheet (2012), Rethink Mental Illness 2011, London

Women who have been abused in childhood are four times more likely to develop major depression in Adulthood
The World Health Report 2001, Mental Health: New Understanding, New Hope Geneva: World Health Organisation p10, (2001)

People who experienced childhood sexual abuse are almost three and a half times as likely to be treated for psychiatric disorders in adulthood as the general population. They are five times as likely to have a diagnosis of personality disorder.
Spataro J et al, Impact Of Child Sexual Abuse On Mental Health, British Journal Of Psychiatry 184 pp416-21, (2004)

Chapter 5:   Secrets & Lies

The next few months were simply blurred with anger, hate, frustration and loneliness whilst I built up internal defence walls that helped me to personally communicate with members of my family. I was angry that they never realised what had been happening to me. I was angry that they did not know to come to my rescue and protected me. All of my emotions were directed at my mum. Back then I blamed her for leaving me in the care of what she thought was a helping hand whilst she attended to the laundry chores. I blamed her for the whooping she gave me instead of having the foresight to question me about why I had been out of bed that night. Then I blamed her for putting me to lay down with another child who unknowing to her was abusing her child. I now blamed her for not waking up that night over Christmas when I lay close by, losing my virginity to a rape. I was left with a numb feeling in my spirit that did not care about me, or her.

Mum noticed the changes in me, and tried sitting me down on a few occasions to ask why I was behaving the way I was. Even if this was now the time to tell her, having managed to get her attention, I couldn't. I could no longer speak with a civil tongue when she spoke to me and there were many times I lost the ability to find any words to answer her questions at all.

I disliked me. What was it about me that made them do what they did? I began to think it must be something I did to attract this attention. Maybe if I changed, others would change to. Food seemed to be the only thing I had any control over. Mum used to allow me to suggest what I would be cooking for dinner before she arrived home. This became my acquired chores, whilst my eldest sister's chore was cleaning which she appeared to love and also become obsessed about. I liked my chore. It felt like it was the only voice I had that seemed to be heard. I loved creating some of the dishes I had learnt in school and began to add some of those to the family menus. Spaghetti Bolognese, shepherd's pie, quiches or those dishes from our own Caribbean menus, corn beef and rice, fried chicken, rice and peas and macaroni cheese. Cooking seemed to be the only thing I thoroughly enjoyed in the family home. This was the time when I realised I was in control of something. I was allowed to banish anyone who came into the kitchen and into my space and in my way whilst I was cooking. With them out of the way I didn't have to engage and I didn't have to talk if I didn't want to. It was whilst I was in this space I realised I also did not have to eat. Who would know?

When it came to dishing up the food, I would claim I had tasted everything I was cooking and no longer had the appetite to eat anything more. I think mum bought it at first and accepted this from the chef. It was obviously feasible for a while until it came to the meals she had cooked. Then mum would call me to the table along with my brothers and sisters for dinner. I would start by picking at the food on my plate and after only a few mouthfuls would claim I was full. This was not seen as acceptable and on many occasions I was forced to sit at the table for long periods of time and told to eat what had been given to me. The problem I faced was the eating of food now made me feel sick although I could feel and hear my stomach grumble to be fed but my thoughts told me not too. I soon got used to sitting at the table and being in trouble but still I would not allow myself to be forced to eat more than I wanted. I realised I was now in control.

Soon mum had to declare to herself she needed help and made an appointment to take me to see the family doctor. I clearly remember her delivering the catalogue of concerns she had faced to get me to eat when we sat in front of this male doctor. He got up and walked around his desk that separated his chair and ours and stood in front of me requesting I looked up to the ceiling. With one finger he pulled down the bottom lid of one eye, repeated the same with the other and then returned back behind his desk. 'She is iron deficient for sure and no doubt anaemic and possibly could become anorexic if she keeps this up' he continued as he wrote out my prescription then looked back at my mum and said, 'looks like she has a bit of an eating disorder so I am going to give her iron tablets and send her for blood tests. I'm also going to give her some flavoured nourishment drinks which will help to replace what she has lost and should start to build up her appetite again.' I realised this gave me more reasons for not finishing my food and an excuse to replace my chewing with boxes and boxes of this milk shake flavoured juices.

My relationships at school were positive. I had a large pool of friends and was popular and confident amongst the different groups I socialised with. I actually had great social skills and did not lack the confidence to project my voice, my confidence, my humour or my likability with these large groups of friends. I certainly was not timid and was not afraid to stand up and defend myself, or any of my friends even if it meant I had to fight it out with either gender. Here, the sexual origin of my peers did not appear to hinder my communication with them. I simply loved being in their company. I realised that being amongst my friends somehow felt as if I had the ability to block out the past, the present and the pain. I concluded that this was because my friends had time for me.

My best friend Samantha became my soul mate. Whenever something upset her it would upset me too. I spent as many days as I could in the week sneaking off to the estate she lived on in Southfields, which happened to be in the opposite direction I should had been taking to go home. I knew mum wouldn't arrive home until 6.30pm or the latest would have been 7pm. This gave me a few hours to play with after school and hang out with Samantha and our peers who also lived around those estates before I would have needed to head home and complete the cooking of the evening meals. I would often make it back just in time to cook something as quickly as I could before mum came in the door to question where I'd been or why I was cooking so late. A few times my eldest sister grassed me up but there was always an explanation to be given that did not include going over to Southfields to hang out.

One day at the end of the PE session in the school gym my emotions overcame me and I felt panicked. For those few minutes my mind was telling me to give up because the burden of the emotional pain felt too much to handle. I could hardly hear any of the instructions being given by the PE teacher as most the girls were leaving the gym and exchanging with each other loud shouts of banter amongst the two teams who had been competing in the games. Plus, some of the spectators were joining in by egging them on. I stood on the spot and suddenly began crying. These were silent tears. I realised just there and then that I truly had had enough and I wanted all this pain to stop right this minute. I moved toward the climbing apparatus mounted along the length of one side of the school gym and began to climb them heading towards the overhead balcony which over looked the gym some hundred and fifty foot or more above ground level. I could faintly register the voices below me asking me what I was doing. I ignored them and continued to climb. When I reached the balcony I stretch over and balanced with one of my hands grabbing hold the wooden top of the railing. I then proceeded to stretch my foot over and lodged it onto the ledge between two metal railings to confirm my balance. My next hand joins in the hold, followed by the remaining foot to ledge. After a deep breath I readjusted my hands and then swung my legs over towards the inside of the balcony landing and rolled over the rest of my body until I was safely able to stand up without any threat of injury and continued my journey to the other side of the balcony by foot for about 50 to 60 yards. On reaching the end I balance my left hand onto the wall, and proceeded to stand on the cemented red plastic chairs that lined that walk like they were my ladders. Next I maneuvered myself to begin my balancing act and climb on the top of the wooden balcony railings with my left hand supporting my balance by clinging on to the slightly raised bricks on the wall, which I think was used for abseiling skills. My mind was telling me to jump.

Shouts began happening below but although I could see people they weren't being fully registered to me in my current state. My eyes felt so blurred from the streams of tears flooding my face that I couldn't really focus on them. My mind was so full with thoughts that I could hardly hear them. 'I could just about make out Samantha's voice shouting 'Beverley what are you doing? Please don't. Bev I love you, don't do this to me.' Samantha had already begun pulling herself up the apparatus as quickly as she could move. 'Bev talk to me please. Tell me.' I tried to concentrate on the task I had at hand but Samantha kept interrupting my thoughts. I could now hear her sniffling as she kept trying to persuade me to come down as she slowly walked closer and closer to me on the balcony. 'Please Bev, I love you so much. I don't want you to hurt yourself or to lose you. You know there is nothing we can't tell each other. Please talk to me.'

In a whispered voice, I responded whilst still focused forward 'Sammy they keep hurting me'

'Who Bev?' she sniffled.

'People' is all I could confirm. By then one of the PE teachers had already began to pull herself up the apparatus and was doing this in a quicker time and pace calculated by mine and Samantha's achievements put together. She must have instructed the children to grab the floor mats, which were about ten yards away from them in one big heap. I suddenly noticed their movement. Each running with mats and throwing them on the floor directly below me and then running back to repeat their actions. 'I can't take anymore Sammy', I told her. As I saw the teacher get closer I turned and looked at Samantha and said 'say nothing' I then turned back and felt my buttocks jerk for the jump.

Just at that point I felt Samantha leap forward and grab the arm that was just about to lead my leap for me. She had managed to clasp most of my upper arm with both hands. I could feel her grip as she squeezed her hands together giving me an instant burning sensation on my biceps. My feet were no longer attached to the top of the wooden railing. They had slipped off and in less time than a breath could be taken I realised I was hanging in a dangle over the ledge. I could feel Samantha trying to pull me back the opposite way. My body had turned forty-five degrees and was no longer facing my audience below but towards the climbing frame. I heard a crack sound in my shoulder and the burning sensation around the part of my arm Samantha was squeezing in her lock hold made me discover in those few vital seconds how strong and desperate she was that day. I was now balancing in her clasp and she now had the responsibility of ensuring I did not take the hundred and fifty foot or so drop that day. She was no longer speaking. She couldn't speak. Instead she looked like she was gritting her teeth when my head tilted upwards. Literally a second later, I felt the PE teacher join in her plight and together they began to pull me back over the balcony as she thanked and praised Samantha.

Samantha hugged me so tightly that I felt my body sink willingly in to hers. I began to sob aloud as I squeezed her back with my hug and whispered in her ear 'you should have let me go Sammy. Promise me you won't tell and I will tell you everything later'

I was taken to the school nurse's office. An hour later mum arrived at the school and I was escorted over to the Head Teacher's office to be handed over to her after the Head himself had spent time speaking to her. That evening mum did ask what this was all about. But I did not answer. Later that night I heard mum's Bajan accent telling someone on the phone, what she told the Head Teacher was that 'she was always the favourite of the father's and became a bit of a handful after we did part.'

Within the next few days I had received a referral to see some psychologist for an assessment at Queen Mary's Hospital in Roehampton. I embraced my appointment with the mind-set that this session was a waste of my time. I knew I couldn't tell what had been happening as the psychologist would just have told my mum and I imagined she would just tell me off for 'chatting our business on street.' Which was always a term I had heard my community and family use all my life. To me, this professional just needed some juice so he could write it down then he would leave me alone. So I gave him trivia. I told him everyone says 'I look like my aunt but my aunt and mum do not always get on and that my mum is always shouting at me. As I expected, I later got told off by mum for chatting these things to the psychologist whose analysis and theory to my problems was that this was some kind of projection issue being caused by my mum's troubled relationship with her youngest sister, aunty Carleen and not about me.

I shared all that had happened in my life with Samantha and she promised not to say anything but urged me to talk to someone who could help. My only response was 'I have.' I was referring to her. It was a relief to finally share this burden with someone else.

My asthma attacks began to get worse which increased my visits to the doctors or calling of an ambulance to take me to the hospital for nebulizer treatments so they could rush some oxygen into my lungs through my tightly squeezed airway. It did not help that I had secretly started smoking both cigarettes and cannabis only six months earlier or had started to steal some of my grandmother's prescription medication drugs which were so easily accessible and stored on shelves on the first floor landing of her home just outside the bathroom door and in her bedside cabinet. I was now popping pills. I hadn't really a clue what I was taking. The only thing I knew is I felt psychologically better just for doing it. I felt like I was in control and the world didn't matter. Some of the powdery tablets made my head feel light but I found the capsules tended to upset my tummy. Probably might have been because I didn't eat very much anyway. All I knew is I definitely didn't need the world because it had shown me it didn't need me for anything good.

I was almost fifteen years.

What makes people become addicted?

Drug dependency is a complex health disorder with social causes and consequences. No single factor can predict whether or not a person will become addicted to drugs. Risk for addiction is influenced by a person's personality, social environment, biology and age or stage of development. The more risk factors an individual has, the greater the chance that taking drugs can lead to addiction. The International Statistical Classification of Diseases and Related Health Problems (ICD-10) defines dependency as: 'A cluster of behavioural, cognitive, and physiological phenomena that develop after repeated substance use and that typically include a strong desire to take the drug, difficulties in controlling its use, persisting in its use despite harmful consequences, a higher priority given to drug use than to other activities and obligations, increased tolerance, and sometimes a physical withdrawal state.' This definition underpins current UK and most drug treatment policy approaches in the Western world.

Facts & Figures, Frequently Asked Questions, National Treatments Agency for Substance Misuse, NHS, London, www.nta.nhs.uk/facts-faqs.aspx

Chapter 6:   Wesley

Wesley my friend from school became fond of me, and my company. He often stopped me for a chat during the school break times and would increasingly make his interest in me clearer when I went to visit the estates in Southfields after school or whenever he heard I was staying over at

Samantha's on a Friday evening; whenever mum allowed it. I like him and he made me laugh. He had so much banter for everyone he came in contact with. He was never pushy with me and seemed to want nothing from me in return, except to a sit down, talk and sometimes let him place one of his arms around my shoulders as if he was giving me a buddy cuddle. One day whilst we were standing at a bus stop on Putney Bridge he asked me out. That was a nice moment, like someone now wanted me. It wasn't long before I realised he actually did loved me and I too began to love him back.

It was about six weeks into our relationship that he noticed tons of pills of all different sizes and colours in my handbag. He questioned me intensely, shooting questions after questions at me about why I had them and whose names were on the bottles. I made up a few answers but for some reason he saw through them and told me I was lying. He began nagging me and nagging me. I suddenly became frustrated and began to cry. But he continued his nagging and suspiciously telling me that I was not telling all. He was making me dizzy in my answering and not allowing me to think. That was always his technique when he was in banter with anyone but this time he had more authority in his approach. He finally achieved his goal and I broke down crying and began blurting out what had been happening to me since I was eight, right up to the point of my cousin Neville whom he knew. He promised me not to say or do anything. His anger showed by the pulse beating at the side of his head, so I had to make him promise me again he would not confront Neville about what I had told him. I pleaded with him to give me the tablets back, which he had removed from my handbag.

'No Beverley,' the tone of his voice was firm and I immediately knew I had a battle on my hands.

'Please Wesley?' I sounded like I was begging.

'What! Are you hooked on these Beverley?'

58

'No I'm not but I want them back'

'Why?' He was starting to irritate me and I immediately knew that getting them back was not going to be easy

'Please Wes? Just give them back'

'They're not yours, so why do you need them back.' He could already tell by my agitation that this was a bigger issue than having just found them in my bag.

'Just give them back. Please. For fuck sake'

'Don't swear at me Beverley or raise your voice. Have you ever witnessed me doing that to you?'

'No. Sorry. Can I have them back please?'

'Are you hooked?' He quizzed.

'No don't be stupid Wes. Of course I'm not. I just want them back' I tried my hardest to sound persuasive but I could see he was not going to let go of this one.

'How long have you been taking these?'

All I could think was damn Wesley, why the hell did you have to find them. 'Not long' I responded.

'You're lying your arse off.' Wesley gave me direct eye contact. I felt so embarrassed.

'I'm not'

'Yeah you are and you know it.' He saw straight through me. 'I can't give you them back Beverley.' Immediately I saw red and tried to jump and grab my stash from his hands. Wesley stepped back and lifted his hands in the air. 'Yeah and your telling me your not hooked'

'I'm not. I just want them back and you're just playing the arse' I tried to defend myself from his accusations of me being some kind of junkie'.

'Yes you are. You're hooked. Look how your eyes look like you get possessed by the devil and you want to kill me.' He mocked and laughed. 'What are you going to start having some kind of shakes if you don't get your shot?'
'Don't be stupid Wesley'

'So why do you want them back?' Wesley simply wasn't going to give in. This was him all over. Whenever he had a point to prove because of someone else's foolishness or unthought-of actions. He would simply mock the life out of them with banter.

'They are not mine. I had to pick them up for my gran'

'You damn liar'

'They are my gran's.'

'So how come you have them?'

'She left them at our house and I was meant to deliver them to her'

'That's a whole heap of cobs-wallop and you know it.' Wesley was never going to buy anything other than the truth.

'Ok, I stole them. You satisfied?'

'Why?'

'Damn Wesley, are you going to give me them or not?'

'Answer the question?'

'There's nothing to answer. Are you giving me them back or not?' I decided I had enough and stood up from the cold wall I sitting on, near his flats and decided I was ready to leave.

'Where do you think you're going Miss Beverley? I have not finished with you yet. Sit back down.' As he sat down he pulled me to sit back down.

'Well I have finished talking' I responded and turned my back with the intension of walking off

Wesley took hold of my arm and pulled me back to him. 'Beverley, this is serious. Sit down. You can't be popping no pills. I bet you don't even know what shit you're taking either. How long have you been doing this?'

'Not long' I tried to sound convincing.

'You can't even be honest about it can you? I asked you how long have you been taking these?'

I shrugged my shoulders whilst looking down at the ground.

'Look at me' Wesley responded but I did not move my head from looking at the ground, so he lifted up my chin and said again in such a loving voice, 'Beverley, look at me please.'

I rolled my eyes up to his eye level and said 'What?'

'How long have you been taking them?' His whole demeanour had changed as he placed by arms lovingly around my neck.

'I don't know Wesley.'

'You do know. Did you start this week? Last month? Last year? When?' This line of questions was so Wesley. He was never going to put it to rest until he got all the answers to all his questions answered.

'Wes, I really don't know'

'What are you telling me you been on them that long you can't remember? What is it years?'

'Don't be stupid. No it's not been years'

'So, how long?'

'Months, I think.'

'You think?'

'Wesley, you're making me feel dizzy. I don't want to talk about this anymore.'

'I don't care if you don't want to talk about it. You're are going to talk about it'. There was almost a chuckle in his voice. I knew he was serious. He was never going to let me put it to rest, unless I came clean with him

'Wes, I truly don't know how long I've been on them. It could be four months it could be eight.'

'Or it could be a year, right?' He responded sharply.

'No it's not been a year'

'How do you know? You can't even remember how long you've been on them' His questions were irritating me.

'I think it's been four'

'If it was four months you would have said that confidently straight away. You know it's been longer. You know I ain't giving them back to you right?' I again went to turn around to storm off but Wesley used his legs to trap me in between them so that I could not turn or walk away. 'Where do you think you're going? I told you I have not finished with you yet. Anyhow, when have you ever seen me turn my back on you and storm off? Cut that out, right now.' That last comment got my attention. He was right, he had never done that to me ever before. I felt my body become less tense and less defensive and I knew he noticed it too. 'That's better.'

It sounded like he was mocking me again so I rolled my eyes up at him and gave a smug grin. 'Can I get them back Wes?'

'You really haven't got the foggiest about what you're taking, do you? You have to stop taking these Beverley.'

'I will' I tried again to sound convincing.

'I know you will because I'm not having you turn yourself into a junkie and you're already trying to put up a fight like you need a fix'

'No I'm not.' Damn cheek is all I could think.

'Yes you are and you know it.'

'How do they make you feel when you take them?'

'I don't know' I tried to seem unknowledgeable on the effects.

'Yes you do. How do they make you feel?'

'Sometimes, light headed, sometimes mellow and sometimes spacey best of all it helps me forget everything' I decided to confess.

'So how does it feel when you don't take them?'

'Why are you asking me all these questions? I don't feel any thing.'

'What do you mean you don't feel anything? Sure you do. I know you're taking nuff of them. Of course you get withdrawal symptoms. What is this agitation about then? Is it a withdrawal symptom or a side effect of the drug? What, are you going to have shakes too?' He laughed.

'You're always mocking' I accused.

'I ain't mocking you. Answer. How does it make you feel when you don't take them?'

'I don't know'

'Yes you do' he crossed examined me. 'What, have you been taking them for a year without any breaks?'

'I did not say I was taking them for a year. Stop trying to put words in my mouth.' He laughed again. I think this time it was because I was as sharp as him under his investigation.

'Again I ask, how does it make you feel when you stop taking them?'

'I don't know.'

'Beverley answer the question.'

'I don't know. Maybe a little shaky, sometimes I get a mild headache and sometimes my stomach or my chest feels tight.'

'Are any of those happening now?'

'No. You're just pissing me off'

'Cut out the language Miss'

'Sorry but you're winding me up'

'You're not wound up. You just feel like this because I found them'

'And because you won't give them back'

'Seriously Beverley, you can't be taking these anymore'

Wesley agreed to return a few of the tabs only because I had threatened that I will get more anyway and that day. He considered me, as I having a problem and it probably wasn't until that point that I too discovered I had.

The next day when we met up he told me to give him all the tablets I had with me in my bag. 'Why? Why bring that up again? Don't be dragging this up every time I see you' I tried to stall him in a battle of questions but his nagging and firmness was no match for whatever I came back with. There were indeed more than he had given back to me the previous day in my bag.

He held the tablets cupped into both hands and placed them into his pockets and put his hand inside his jacket pocket and took out one tiny small yellow tablet in his hand. 'What's that? How can you take everything I had and give me that?' I felt cheated.

'I nicked it. It's Valium. I'm going to check and confiscate any tablets I find on you for one of these from now on and then I will reduce this one to half and then none'. As he spoke I looked in his face. He was serious about promising to lose his temper with me if he ever found me popping scrap like this again, once I stopped taking these ones which he said will happen in the next week or two. As bad as this exchange may have sounded, he actually probably saved my life with his monitoring my withdrawal with immediate effect.

The atmosphere at home was not inviting. Looking back, my mum must have been exhausted trying to cope with this emotionally disturbed child. But I didn't care. I had enough coping with what I thought was emotionally displaced adults in my world. They were all simply blind or just wicked.

I never spoke to Neville about that Christmas night and he never ever spoke to me about it. We just carried on as normal. Now and again he would steal a second when there was no one around to hear him declare in a whispering voice that I was his favourite cousin or reminding me that if anyone ever hurt me I should tell him. He just simply acted like my big cousin again. I tried to put the relationship with Neville into some kind of intellectual perspective. Everyone loved him and no one would have ever believed me anyway. After all he was one of the first-borns and I wasn't. He was not the troubled one and I was known as the handful. Neville continued coming to my defence whenever there was a need, especially when I felt under attack by gran or mum. For that alone I had to love him but hated my cousin for taking my virginity. This was something I would never be able to forget. This was going to live with me for the rest of my life. I would never be able to reclaim this back and give it to the one I loved or be able to experience a special moment like one of those in the movies when a person makes one of those important transitions of their life from childhood to adulthood. He had taken this all away and it was now gone forever. Over the coming year Neville moved on and went to live with other relatives.

Nothing changed following that day in the gym. The discussion of my suicide attempt never reappeared again after that day between my mum or any member of the family with me. It was like everything was swept under the carpet and back to normal we go. I heard my mum on many occasions sharing her opinions with her friends or family members on the telephone just outside of my bedroom door. Mum would provide updates of what had happened and never failed to let them know how exhausted she was. I would simply listen until I fell asleep with tears streaming down my face and anger building in my heart.

It really did not take me that long to withdraw from the tablet dependency I had developed. The first couple of weeks I felt a little agitated but the tender love and determination Wesley surrounded me with felt like I was being nurtured off the addiction. I'm sure this played a big part in my accepting the withdrawal. I began to feel a sense of happiness and worth within me. I realised I had someone in my life who truly wanted me whole. It made everything feel so much easier and worth it now.

Slowly, Wesley began coming around to our house. Mum seemed to have liked him at first especially when she knew his parents were from our home country, Barbados. I was so glad. For a few weeks he was so very welcomed in our home. Then one day mum just upped and changed on me. Her tone when she spoke about him changed. She would tell me that he would have to leave the house and the time was often around 6pm on a Saturday. She would embarrass me and tell me to go bathe and get ready for bed. Before long she declared at the top of her voice to me that she thought he was a predator. 'Don't think I haven't heard how he has a child when he was only 15 years old'. Soon enough her comments went on to 'I know he looking for some fresh blood huh? Well not here' If only she knew, he had made it clear to me that he would not hurt me or take advantage of me like all those other people in my life. And he never did.

My anger towards my mum began to raise its head again. I saw her as the threat taking away someone I truly loved and the only person who showed me real love without taking any advantage of me. Wesley kept telling me to remain quiet and be humble whenever I told him mum had a go at me. He promised we would see each other, but we needed to win my mum over properly. That I thought would never happen.

I spent as much time in Southfields as I could. I became an active member of a youth club there and before long I volunteered to help out in their girl's group sessions for the ten to thirteen year olds. It felt so wonderful to be valued and have a role to play in something so worthy. My jobs consisted of helping to promote the session; helping the youth workers to set up the rooms with the resources that were to be used from 4pm when the session opened; doing the registration list and taking subs at the front door as the girls arrived; and help to encourage the girls to take part in the discussion groups and activities. I simply loved what I was doing with great and growing passion. The discussion sessions were so exciting. This created opportunities to speak about issues that I knew nobody ever spoke to me about. No one ever asked me to identify those relationships that were ok and those that weren't. No one ever explored drugs, peer pressure, isolation, anger or any of those things. I felt I had so much to offer and give back to these young girls. I began to develop a new and personal mission in my life and that was to stop abuse happening to other young girls and young people on the whole; or at least I could be aware of the signs and I would be prepared to rescue them if I had too. I realised that whilst I was doing this work I was no longer feeling like a victim. I now had a purpose and a vision for my life. My only problem was I had to depend on my ability to hide my activities from mum or be able to gain her approval whenever I asked to stay at Samantha's house so that I could attend the youth club without fear of having to leave early to return home on time.

Life at home kicked back into favouritism. I was nearly sixteen years old and my sister was only one year older. She had no difficulties inviting her new boyfriend Gerald over, having him stay late until the early hours of the morning without fear of mum kicking off and kicking him out. It wasn't long before he was able to stay over and ended up between my sister and me in the double bed that we shared.

One night I awoke to this sleeping arrangement with his hand going up my thigh underneath my nightdress. I panicked but this time I knew I could not lay there. As with all previous times, I still couldn't say a word. Fear simply took my voice away. But this time was different. I felt an overwhelming refusal to stay. I began pretending to be stirred as if I was having a bad dream. I began stretching, tossing and turning as if I was waking up. His hand quickly moved away. This I felt gave me the excuse to sit up and look around as if to imitate a 'what was that', impression and then take myself out of the bed and head to the toilet. I was convinced my actions looked natural. I wasn't in the toilet for that long before I felt my body turn from cold to freezing. All I knew was, I was not returning back into that bed. 'No-way, no-how' is all I kept turning over in my head. So I decided to return into the room and collected myself a blanket, which was stored in the top part of the wardrobe and took myself off to the sitting room to sleep out the rest of the night. I remember laying there uncomfortable in the chair blaming both my mum for allowing my sister's boyfriend to lay in our bed and also my sister for having him there.
In the morning, he got up and left. I went to my sister and decided for the first time ever, that I was going to tell. 'I woke up last night because your boyfriend had his hand under my night dress trying to touch my private parts.'

I could not believe the response I heard back, 'what did you do to cause him to do that?'

How could she have asked that? What the hell did she think I could have done? How bloody dare her. He attacks me and she asks what I did. Now I was convinced everyone was sick. He stayed many times after that night but she must have taken on board what I had said as she put herself in the middle. I dropped a complaint about him staying over to mum but she never seemed to listen and I think she thought I was trying to get Wesley to be welcomed in the house and she made it clear that she wasn't going to welcome that idea, so she simply ignored what I had to say.

Time sped up and before I realised my sixteenth birthday came and went. There was no party it was a quiet occasion celebrated with a cake to share amongst my brothers and sisters and some calls from family relatives. Soon after my birthday I managed to get myself my first ever part time job down Putney High Street in a supermarket called Presto. It sold aisles and aisles of freezer food. This job opened me up to so much potential as I was now in the position where I could save up the money I was earning from the four to six hours a week working as a cashier and one day I would have enough to leave home and find a place of my own to live in.

That day was to come two months later and did not turn out the fairy tale way I had fantasised. Instead, one morning mum told me to wash my sister's dishes because she had worked the night before and was tired. That made me furious. 'Damn that' I thought and attempted to defend myself with, 'when I work, I still have to do the dishes.' My argument was not unreasonable. I had always completed the dishes on the days mum had rotas between us sisters so why should I have to do it on her night, as well. I was absolutely sick of this favouritism rubbish. There was no fairness in it. Well I decided I was no longer playing any of their games. I was sick of them and I was done with it so I made up my mind there and then, not another one!

Mum could see my stubbornness had sunk in and she became furious. She began to bellow threats at me just before she left to go to work that morning, 'make sure they are done Beverley before I get home if not pack your bags and go.'

All I could think was 'Damn you. You will never have to ask me twice.' Whilst she was gone I packed and left.

I was sixteen years, two months and three days old.

Homelessness

Key points:
• All forms of homelessness, including youth homelessness, are on the rise.
• The biggest cause of homelessness for young people is being told to leave the family home by their parents. Other common causes are leaving care and being unable to pay rent.
• Young homeless people often do not get the help they need from local authorities or formal support services. Instead, they get by in hidden homelessness situations such as rough sleeping and squatting.
• Young homeless people are considerably more vulnerable than the overall homeless population. For example, 51% have been excluded from school, 40% have experienced abuse at home and 33% self harm.
• 30% have been in care, suggesting that the care system is not offering them the support they need.
• Young homeless people go to desperate measures to avoid sleeping rough, including committing a crime or resorting to sex work to get a roof over their head.
• Urgent action and early intervention is needed to prevent young homeless people developing higher needs and falling into long term homelessness.

Crisis Research briefing: Young, hidden and homeless (April 2012), CRESR for The hidden truth about homelessness, PDF pg1.

Chapter 7:   Sofa surfing

My invitation to temporarily stay at friends in Southfields did not go down well with Wesley. He tried telling me how much worse things were going to get if I stayed away from home. He tried to convince me that as unhappy as I was, my unhappiness was about to get worse. He also kept reminding me of the fact that the welcome for me kipping at our mutual friend's house on her children's bedroom floor would wear out very soon. He did his best to deter the choices I had made by providing me with as many horror stories as he could about how people will take advantage of me knowing I was living on the streets.

I realised that my return to school to attend the sixth form was now no longer the choice I had always envisaged all those times I stood outside that block knowing one day I would be allowed in there and my brother and younger sister would have to one day wait by the lower stairs if they needed to come over to get me, just like I had to do with Neville, my cousin and then with my eldest sister when they attended there. But this was no longer an option, as it would result in mum being able to find me and the school getting involved.

I seemed to have a good relationship with the store manager where I worked so I let him know I had left home and gave him a new and very temporary address. I was able to increase my working hours as I did not have much money and I began to be fully conscious of my need to be able to provide for and support myself after I enquired in the office, which was tucked away at the back of the shop. I also requested that if anyone should come into the store asking for me or enquiring when I was next on shift that they were not to tell them. I stayed there a further five weeks and decided that the stress of being put regularly on the cashier at the front of the shop was simply too much stress and risked me getting caught by mum or a members of my family and even family friends. So I worked out my notice of a week and left.

I had managed to save just over three thirds of my wages and had spent the rest of it helping to buy food for my friend's house. I only ate toast and coffee in the morning and she provided me with an evening meal. She was surprised how little I ate and wasn't aware that I had been starving my stomach of food for just over a year now. However I was more conscious about helping myself in the kitchen as I didn't want her to feel like I was a burden that she has to ask me to leave before I sorted myself out. On the last day at work, I got my friend to come into the shop and come over to my cashier when she filled her trolley with whatever she needed. When she came to my counter I did not tap in to the cashier any of the meats, or expensive items. To be honest it was probably less than a quarter of the items that got rung in. I was frightened, even though I had done this a couple times before; like then, my conscious was riddled with fear, guilt and shame at the idea of being caught for theft. This was stealing; there was no other way of looking at it. The last thing I needed was to be frog-matched out of the shop by police. That would have also sent me back home disgraced and prove I was unable to manage out in this big wide world on my own. This shopping although appeared to feel like a blessing to my older friend was actually my only way of being able to contribute financially towards the household for the next few weeks to come until I could sort out my next plan. The money I had saved, I treated it like it was gold dust and already became conscious about my need to budget and manage what I had but I knew it was not going to last forever.

My friend advised me to let social services or the unemployment office know that I am estranged from my family and living on different people's floors every night and have no money. I went along to the address for unemployment office that she gave me. The outside of the building looked old and the entrance stunk of stale urine and alcohol. There was a queue of what looked like real homeless men and women in not so clean clothes either sitting or crouching in the smelly entrance smoking and talking; and along the long plastic and metal benches that lined the walls as I walked inside the building in to an almost open plan room. I couldn't work out where or what I was supposed to do now. There were cubicles booths with people sitting on benches that were cemented into the floor on one side and the staff looked like they were imprisoned by these high thick plastic sheets, which divided them between the people who were talking to them. There wasn't any reception to go to. It looked like I was the youngest person in the building.

I turned to someone sitting on the chair and said 'where's the queue please?'

'Get yourself a ticket from over there and take a seat. Hopefully you'll get out of here before it closes'

She was right. When I left they had to unbolt the door to let me out. This place was the worse place I had ever walked into in my life. I felt so lost, nervous and the reality of my plight was starting to really hit home. I was advised that they would need to contact my mum to confirm that I was estranged. I said if you do that then I might as well leave now and continue to sleep on friends' floors or live on the streets as I could not and would not go back there. With that she began to fill in forms. The advisor informed me if I went down to the careers office and signed up for a course then I would be able to get a training allowance which would be paid at a slightly higher rate because I was estranged from my family. That took all day to hear that. Now I would have to do this all over again tomorrow when I visited the careers office.

The next day I sensed urgency to my situation and made sure I got to the career's office half hour before it opened so that I could be the first person. There must have been a handful of people there on my arrival that thought the same thing. Most courses had already started back but I had heard from friends that some colleges might even enroll me in up to mid October, if I was lucky. I began to feel overwhelmed about my future in case I could not get onto a course that would take care of what my future would look like over the next year. Plus without the course I would have no access to money. I realised I couldn't be a homeless or unemployed statistic that I thought others expected me to be, so as soon as the doors opened I rushed over to the boards and literally accepted the first possible course I saw being advertised. The course was in Fulham and literally only ten minutes walk from where my grandparents lived. However I had consciously reasoned with myself that where the study college was situated none of my family would walk that way and I didn't need to go toward the busy main road to make my way back to Southfields. Instead I would walk the opposite way even if it added on an extra forty minutes to my journey and meant I had to walk through two parks and through some backstreets to get to the next town. So I decided at least it would be relatively discreet.

I couldn't have been so wrong. The day I registered I noticed our very close family friend who was more like a big sister to me, working in the admin office. That was a truly uncomfortable and shocking experience. I tried running passed the administrators office every time I came in and out of the building all that day and the rest of the week so that she wouldn't see me. Most times she would call out my name even though I had already made it past the door and would call me back. When I returned to her, most of her conversation would be same, 'so what? You can't say hello?' or 'have you been to visit your mum yet?'

On the Friday of the first week Arah Samuels the welfare officer at the college came into my class and asked the teacher to excuse me for a while. I really had no idea why. On entering her office my queries were revealed. My mum was sitting there. She must have set up this mediation meeting with the welfare officer. My heart began pounding and I felt sick and frightened. On first glance mum looked thinner, paler, sad, hurt and distraught. I could not look her in the eyes and turned to look at the welfare officer for help. Instead she invited me to take a seat on one of the two swivel chairs on the other side of her at the end of her small rectangle shaped office. I chose the chair furthest away. Arah broke the silence and began to introduce what this reunion was about by telling me that my mum had got in touch and told her that I had left home and had wanted the opportunity to come and see me to find out what was wrong. I was comforted at her next words when she told me she would have to stay in the office unless I preferred she didn't. All I could think was no way can I face mum on my own, so I asked her to stay. She then turned to mum and asked her if she would like to start off the talking. My mind was racing and trying to catch up all at the same time.

Mum's voice trembled as she began to speak. Her first words were a direct question 'are you coming home?'

Immediately my thoughts kicked in and instructed me not to look at her and not to become weak from any of her pleas. I may not be living in the best of environments right now I answered my thoughts with, but I was sure that no way did I want to return home. As far as I was concerned, I was walking away from years of abuse that she knew nothing about.

'No, I'm not coming back.' Until that day when I became defiant about the washing up, I had never really disobeyed mum's orders. But this day I knew I had to be strong and do the same again.

Mum's fears, worry and stress all seemed to turn in one swoop into an immediate form of anger as she stood up giving me those piecing looks. That made my hot and clammy body begin to perspire underneath my clothing that I could feel drops of sweat rolling from my armpits down the side of my body. Mum began to raise her voice as she said 'you ungrateful child' along with a few more words which I did not catch as my head was stuck on those words of me being an ungrateful child.

As quickly as she said it she simply stood up, turned her body towards the door and reached out to pull the handle of the door towards her, then proceeded to walk straight out slamming the door behind her. My heart was pounding even harder but at the same time I had this sense in my spirit that I had won a battle. I realised I no longer needed to stay in hiding. I was now officially free and I had stood up for me.

Arah was now aware of my plight and that afternoon she told me she had been making calls to landlords who had advertised in a couple papers and had managed to get me an appointment that day to go and view the first bed-sit which was in Tooting and gave me a form to complete for housing benefit and scheduled me in for the following day to finish complete it with her once I found a place to live. That day, I left my classes and headed over to view the first bed-sit on the list. As soon as I saw it, I took it. I didn't fall in love with it, I just reasoned with myself that now I had my own place and my own haven and that no one will ever abuse me again.

Wesley and I finished about a week later. I was devastated. He was the one person that had shown love without taking advantage of me in any shape or form. He finished with me in anger. He went on and on and on about me needing to go and visit my mum and put things right and I had left his home that particular day forced into accepting the decision he had planted in my mind to go and see her. However I did not have the courage, so spent the next ninety minutes or so talking to one of Wesley's sister's male friends directly underneath Wesley's flat on the estate in Southfields, whilst the friend was fixing parts on his BMW car.

Maduka was of Indian descent and had the nickname around the estate as Spooks. He was a polite, quiet and a trendy looking young man who simply did not fit in amongst our peers on the estate. He always reminded me of a 'wannabe' which was one of those people from a different culture who wanted to be another culture, just not his own. He simply didn't fit in on this estate. I was convinced he was probably a middle class Asian guy whose family lived in a big house, had several shops, which were all family run, and his dad wore a turban and his mum wore saris.

Spooks was quite charming to speak to, although he didn't have bags of wit or humour going for him but seemed to give a refreshing response to questions asked of him. He didn't answer with jokes, silly comments, big talks or even innuendos. He simply just asked and answered questions and before I realised it I was standing there longer than I had expected to, simply talking away the early evening. He was quite interesting really. I had seen him around many times and had never before had a proper conversation with him. After Spooks had completed his repairs he asked if I wanted to go on the road with him, as he needed to test-drive the part of the motor he had just fixed in his car. I agreed not reading anything more into it. Unfortunately and by life's fluke chance as we were driving back towards Southfields from Clapham Common we stopped at a red traffic light and heard the car next to us hooting its horn. We both turned to look and when my eyes focused on the passengers and the driver I could have died where I sat. 'Shit, shit, shit' was all I could bellow out as I tried to duck down but the seat belt had me locked in the upright position. There were at least four guys and Wesley from the estates in Southfield, sitting in the car. I didn't even think to wind down the window and say hi back. All I could think is he's not going to believe a word I say.

Back on the estate whilst I was still standing talking to Spooks, Wesley walked up to us and looked at Spooks and said 'keep her'. I couldn't believe my ears, he was handing me over to someone else. He then turned and walked away. I tried walking after him but he firmly and angrily said 'Go away Beverley. Move from me.' Wesley made up his own mind that I was having an affair with Spooks as much as I tried; he refused to even acknowledge my existence.

I had lost so much joy in my heart. Spooks stuck around for about four or five months having accepted that I was now his. For some reason, I didn't know what to say. Initially I think for him, it was to provide that shoulder for me to cry on but for me I had internalised and accepted that I had been handed over to him and did not quite know how to challenge that decision or thought. So simply found myself trying to accept him officially as my boyfriend and I said nothing to deter that from happening.

Spooks' was a good guy. Actually a gentleman, but he annoyed the hell out of me with his niceness. He drove me everywhere; picked me up from everywhere and jumped to my needs even when I blinked. I actually felt like I couldn't breathe. He timed everything just to make sure he was where I said I would be to the very second I said it. If I said I wanted to leave to go to the shops, he drove or walked me there. If I said I was going to visit friends he dropped me there and returned at least five minutes before the time I said I would leave there by and would be waiting patiently in his car. At the age of nearly seventeen years I did not know how to appreciate this. I did not feel free or carefree. Our relationship felt robotic like it was on a timer. I also began to feel like a manipulator as I shared my plans that entailed my day and he would immediately juggle whatever he had on around my schedule. Spooks did not work because he said is parents gave him an allowance plus he received regular money from some investment funds that his parents had paid into since he was a child.

In such a short time we managed to experience prejudice and cultural problems from strangers. I remember one like occasion when we were standing in McDonalds when a group of young black men surrounded Spooks and asked him what he was doing with one of their women. The bloody cheek is all I could think and jumped in front of Spooks ready to fight his fight with my boldness. 'Who the hell tell you seh, I'm your woman? You need to go find yourself one of them and leave me and mine alone. About you ah speak for me.' Not even I realised I could be so brave. Even though the words sounded confrontational my body language was showing them my claim to my decision as I put my arms around Spook's waist firmly and lovingly. They kissed their teeth at me as I left with my words dangling in the air. I knew they saw me as a sell out. Damn fools, is all I could think. Spooks literally said nothing throughout the whole conflict so as we walked down the road back to my bed-sit. I began cussing him about being such a wimp and telling him how I nearly got my arse busted for him. From there on, I realised this man could not protect me if some other man came to hurt me again.

Our ending came as quickly as our relationship began. I found out he had been caught committing a burglary with a few of the guys in Southfields. I was so angry. I became emotionally and verbally abusive to him for his foolishness by calling him names starting with, 'you fool!'

Spooks tried everything possible to avoid going to court and went as far as eating rat poison that would see the case deferred for less than a month to see him recover in hospital. My annoyances grew with him because I saw his wounds as being self-inflicted. So I had no sympathy what so ever with his attention seeking behaviour and added to his burdens when I read an attempted suicide letter he had written to me to say good-bye. My only response to his surprise was, 'if you can't do the time, you shouldn't have done the crime'. I also dug in deeper and told him 'if you were attempting suicide then you would have done it.' I was angry with him 'how could you think of using my bed-sit to do this? That is totally unforgivable and a disgusting thing to do to me. Personally, I think you are all out of order, robbing off other people's livelihoods.' I could only imagine, if the little I had, had been taken away from me, how it would have made me feel.

Spooks received about three years for his part as the getaway driver in the burglaries and I went to visit him when I received his first Visiting Order known simply to everyone as a VO. On that visit I told him I did not sign up for prison time so would never be coming back to visit him again and wanted nothing more to do with him. However, it became also an easy decision to make since he was locked up and could not have persuaded me otherwise. I was more worried about my image of being a teenager and living with a criminal boyfriend. Plus, I had met someone new a few weeks into Spooks being held on remand prior to his prison sentence.

I was grateful to Spooks for several achievements whilst knowing him and having him in my life for those short few months. It had made the transition from homelessness to living alone in the bed-sit less daunting. He had supported me in establishing my relationship back with my mother and the wider family and did not leave my side on any visit until I gained my confidence to visit everyone on my own. On those occasions I didn't mind him arranging to pick me up and take me back home. Then there of course was that confrontation I had with those men some months earlier that made me feel courageous and knowing I was able to be articulate and speak up for myself if someone tried to hurt or offended me again.

I had been through so many changes already in the last seven months. From working as a volunteer youth worker; facing homelessness; leaving my job; finding a course; finding a bed-sit; ending my beautiful relationship with Wesley who had made sure I was always protected and safe; being handed over to a new boyfriend who ended up in prison; re-establishing my relationship with my family and now I was about to enter another relationship. By October of that year my life felt on track when I successfully obtained two paid, part-time youth workers post at other youth clubs. I had also completed my first academic year on a course since leaving school and now was enrolled into a new college.

I had settled down into a routine and at the age of seventeen I was paying towards my own rent, supporting all my needs and myself. My bed-sit was my home and indeed the only sanctuary I had but that came often at a cost of defending or protecting my rights and my physical space as a young women living alone.

When I thought nothing else could possibly happen it did. Neville my abusing cousin moved in with our Uncle Royston and his lovely wife Aunty Sandra; and my favourite girl cousin who was more like my younger sister than my cousin; their daughter Emma whom all lived only two roads away from where I lived.

Since being a young child, I had spent many nights, weekends and school holidays sleeping in their last home. They treated me like a favourite niece. I could speak with Aunty Sandra more than any other adult I ever knew and she would never jump to negative conclusions and never saw me as being any trouble. I believed she knew I held on to an inner sadness or believed something was not right. She always spent so much time nurturing me into conversations. I loved her so much I couldn't help clinging to her whenever I saw her. This often resulted in her taking me home with them for a few nights and if I was lucky, longer and I knew she knew that I didn't want to go back home.

I was beginning to have numerous altercations with my landlord who kept missing payments on the gas and electricity bills. This infuriated me knowing that I had paid my rent to him on time. He often sent a couple of heavy set and frightening men to the house to collect rent arrears from my bed-sit neighbours. I lived in a house where 4-6 people and their guests occupied the top half of the house and the ground floor level was always rented out to large families.

On one occasion I went up to my landlord's shop to complain about the loss of electricity when I awoke one morning. As I entered the shop the landlord was standing behind the till so I walked over to him to make my complaint. 'Good morning Mr. Chughtai' I always stuttered when I say his name simply trying to concentrate so that I don't get it wrong. 'Why is there no electricity?'

His only response to me was, 'get out of my shop'
'I beg your pardon. I asked why there isn't any electricity.'

In a truly angry voice he shouted, 'get out!'

'How dare you speak to me like that? I will report you to the housing ombudsman and council if you don't sort it by today. You have tenants in that house and one of them is disabled and uses a wheelchair so you better have it back on today.'

With that, he shot from around his counter and punched me in my stomach. I fell to the floor in absolute pain and totally feeling winded. He wife ran from the back of the shop shouting 'stop, stop' and reached out her hands to help pick me up. I was swaying and my head felt like it was about to explode as I held my breath in to hold in the pain. She pulled my arched over body to my feet and immediately turned me around to face the door and proceeded to push me straight out of the shop still in pain with tears flooding down my face only to tell me, 'go home.'

I could not believe what just happened. The man assaulted me and his wife just put me out on the street and leaves me. I was in so much pain. I began to walk but I felt dizzy and scared at the same time. I decided to try and sit down on one of the walls to try and gather myself together. Damn that hurt bad.

I began walking having made up my mind to call the police. But the nearest phone box ended up being only a block away from the police station so I decided to walk there. I had to pass the end of my uncle Royston's house. As I peeped down his road I could see he was high up on a ladder painting the front of his house. I stood there couched down behind a car for what felt like ages still trying to nurse my pain and so desperately not wanting to get caught passing by, my uncle. What made the situation worse was he looked like he was speaking to a neighbour so was facing in my direction. I decided to go for it and began walking with my head in the other direction to keep myself under cover. As soon as I began walking, my uncle began calling. 'Beverley, Beverley' and as if I didn't hear him, he repeated 'Beverley' at the top of his voice.

I waved back and turned to walk in his direction. Discreetly I tried wiping my eyes and walking in a more upright position. That hurt. I took a deep breath and said 'morning uncle.' I even threw in a smile.

'How you can be walking past and not say hello?'

'Sorry, I was heading somewhere in a hurry'

'Why do you look like you've been crying? What happened?'

Shit. He knows is all I could think and burst out into tears. 'My landlord just punched me in my stomach when I went to his shop to ask him why there was no electricity.'

It was no point lying to him, as I knew I could not pull it off. However I did not expect him to fly down the ladder and pick up a hammer and demand, 'Where is his shop?' Uncle Royston was mad. I had never seen him in a rage and I was now frightened.

'Please Uncle don't. I'm on my way to the police station.'

Uncle Royston dismissed my mission and asked again, 'where is his shop Beverley?'

'The Asian corner shop on Franciscan Road.' With that information, Uncle Royston marched over to his car.

—

85

'Please uncle. I don't want you getting involved. Please. He refused to listen to my pleas and continued walking. 'Aunty Sandra, come quick! Quick Auntie!' She came running to the door. 'Aunty my landlord beat me up and uncle's taking a hammer to him.'

'Royston, Royston, Royston' my uncle refused to turn round to Aunt Sandra's scream. 'Beverley get in the car but don't let him go. I got to grab the key.' She said as she was almost running backwards.

I turned and ran to uncle. Literally ten seconds behind me was aunt and she joined in my pleas in begging uncle to go to the police station instead. 'Shut up' he pelted and broke into silence. Uncle was damn mad and I was damn frightened.

We pulled up outside the shop and uncle didn't even let the car sit for a second when he turned off the engine. He flew open his car door and marched through the doors of this little mini-mart and straight over to the counter where the landlord stood with two customers and proceeded to grab him by the neck and raise up the hammer. Both aunt and I had entered the shop screaming at Uncle to stop and together we was now trying to pull the arm holding the hammer away from the direction of my landlord who had been forced to shuffle up against the back of his wall staring fear back in the eyes.

'Touch my niece again and I will kill you.' In exchange of his threat my uncle lifted his knee and stamped it either into his stomach or his privates. I couldn't quite tell which. 'This is your only warning' and with that he marched right back out of the shop and back into the car.

I have always had a truly close relationship with Uncle Royston, Aunt Sandra and their daughter Emma. There really wasn't anything I couldn't really tell them, except of course that all these people in my childhood had been abusing me, including my cousin who was now living in their house. Having discovered my Uncle's hidden temper, I now knew it would be triggered off to show his love for me if I told the truth. This was something I knew I would not be able to cope with, as it would not have resulted with such a civil outcome and in return I knew my uncle would be penalised by the law and I would never want that.

The incident involving my landlord was reported at the police station with my Aunt present. We were informed that the results of an investigation would have been better for me if I had called them to the scene of the crime instead of walking away. So was notified that it would be logged as a reported crime, which can be used later if anything should happen again.

I spent the next day nursing my wound. My stomach was hurting. I sustained a bruise and had developed pains and cramps inside my stomach and so took myself off to the toilet. I sat there for sometime clutching at my stomach when I heard some strange bubbling sounds coming from my vaginal area followed by tremendous cramps. Something felt like it was passing through my body. I groaned in pain. It was almost an hour later when the pains and sweating subsided a little. I had not passed any urine or stools but some kind of bubbly-matter had fallen into the toilet bowl. I rose up and turned to look at it. It looked almost jelly baby-like and had a drop of blood at one end with this jelly-looking fine string coming off the blood part. I tried to scoop it out of the toilet with the toilet brush but I could not get it to grip the brush. There was nothing else in the bathroom that I could use as a scoop so I decided to flush it away and walk down the bottom of my road to my doctors.

I spoke to the doctor about the assault; the cramps and what I had seen in the toilet by trying to draw a picture of what it looked like. In exchange he gave me a specimen bottle and told me to go to the toilet and fill it with a mid-stream sample of my urine and hand it back to the receptionist and then take a seat. So I did.

87

'Miss Walcott'

I stood up and walked back into the room and sat down. The doctor greeted me with 'Thank you. Ok I am going to first take a pregnancy test and depending on that result will determine the next action.

Pregnancy test! All I could think was, 'Oh my God, please let it be negative'. I had never assumed I would be pregnant as I had been on the pill although I had not always taken it in the period of time expected. My main fear was whose was it? My boyfriend Martin's or Neville's my abusing cousin who had returned into my life to torment me only a few weeks earlier. I felt like I stopped breathing whilst he dipped a strip into the urine and we waited.

'As I suspected from your drawing, you're pregnant. I'm going to send you to the hospital immediately for an ultra sound and further investigation. You may have miscarried and may also have remains of the foetus still in your womb. If you are still pregnant there is slim possibilities it may have been twins but let's get the scan under way first to let us know what's happening.

The scan resulted in the evidence I feared. I was pregnant. The worry was too much to think about. I told Martin I was pregnant but was too embarrassed to face my family and tell them I was. So I made the decision to terminate the pregnancy. Martin was deeply hurt but he also knew I refused to have my mind changed either.
All these events happening in my life and I was only seventeen years old. Not even officially regarded as an adult yet.

For Perry, the opportunity to free himself from the stranglehold of silence that abusers have over their victims has transformed his life. 'Since speaking about the abuse I have experienced a significant change,' he says. 'My mental health has improved and I now feel that I am out of that dreadful hole looking down at it.

Kelly Mattison, Speaking Out acclaim for survivors of childhood abuse, The Guardian Newspaper, Wednesday 25 November 2009

Chapter 8:   No more secrets

The following year of our eighteen birthdays, my best friend Samantha passed away the day after she had given birth to her baby girl; my God-daughter. My world fell apart. Her death affected the realms of my mental wellness and it became a need for me to spend my daytimes for the next six months getting ready for college with my pack lunch in hand but by the time I headed to the end of my road my plans would change. I would decide I needed my best friend instead, so spent each day by her graveside talking to her. I was suffering from bereavement and there was no one who could cushion the blow. My best friend was dead and she had taken my secrets of my child abuse with her, to her early grave. Now there was no one else who knew my plight, except Wesley my ex-boyfriend who was serving a long prison stretch for burglary and had moved on anyhow with his love life. There was no one who could keep me strong when I felt weak. I had lost my two soul mates.

The bereavement triggered the anger and hurt I felt with my own life. Eight months later, I realised I needed help and found myself a counsellor whom I visited every

Thursday. This relationship lasted three years. It took the first four weekly hourly sessions before I could truly begin to open up and spill the hurts. For most of the first three weeks, I simply sat crying and the counsellor sat patiently holding my hand. I could only release the names of the people who had hurt me with some scattered information about the ages I had been. My main focus of those first immediate weeks was attempting to cope with my devastating loss of my best friend Samantha and reduce my nighttime hallucinations and daytime false sightings of her.

My counseling relationship became more of a habitual routine for me and did nothing really to move me on in my ability to cope with the outside world, outside of the room. I simply loved going because I had someone who would listen to me and it was my hour. The techniques used by the counsellor consisted of lots of nodding of her head in acknowledgement of what I shared with her and then choosing to repeat everything I had just told her so that she could check her understanding of what I had been telling her. There were painful moments too. She would have me role play some of the moments of the sexual abuse and then have me confront my invisible abusers. This was never easy and always had me in freeze-mode with floods of tears running down my face by the end of my hour. She would then have about fifteen to twenty minutes to get me composed and escort me to the converted shop's front door, ready for the next awaiting client to be able to start their counselling session on time. I often walked around the corner, which was a residential road and cried myself silly. I learnt the importance of turning up with a pack of tissues in my pocket, just for these moments.

To this day I will never forget my first role-play. Probably that was because I had no one to talk to about it when the incident had taken place during that week and my world and resources again began to fall apart. I had been at my boyfriend's home when someone knocked the door.

Immediately whoever opened the door said 'Hi Miriam. My mum's not home you know.'

Immediately I knew it was my mum at the door and I guessed she had just popped over to say hi to my boyfriends mum. Over the years mum had invited her to some of her parties. After all, both mothers had their children dating each other and my eldest sister and Gerald had already made them grandparents. Mum had walked the few streets from my Grandparents house.

'It's not your mum I came to see. Is Beverley there?'

'Come in' invited the person who opened the door.

'Thank you' mum replied. I had heard my name called so had already begun walking to the door.

'Hi mum' I greeted her. As soon as mum saw me her expression changed.
'What is it you tell Joan?'

'Joan?' I was puzzled thinking, Joan who? 'Sorry?' I said, returning a surprised question.

'Mrs. Peters' she confirmed.

'I haven't seen Aunty Joan'

'You liar' mum accused. I seriously had no idea what she was talking about. Before I could utter a response, I felt her slap me hard across my face.

It was here I seemed to have no recollection of what exactly happened next. I could only assume I flipped. From the position I was being confronted in the hallway, I next recall my boyfriends brothers shouting out my name with objection sounds like 'nah, nah, nah' and saying 'you mustn't do that' 'let go' as they started pulling me off of my mum who was now laying on the stairs underneath me.

I couldn't work out how we got there. Did mum pull me down? Was I trying to get her off me? Was I pulling her hair? Did I attempt to strangle her? I still don't know if I hit her back or I manoeuvred her blows, which were coming one after the other. Did this result in her falling on top of me? However I do remember everyone pulling me up from off her. I truly can't recall those few seconds though. Up until that day, I had never and knew I would never in my life hit my mum again. Regardless of how much she managed to stir up painful feelings for me. I never managed to notice the crimes caused against me, somehow hitting her would have been a bigger and worse crime.

Mum stood up and as quick as she came, she left. I was fuming. How could she come round here and do that? How could she shame me in front of everybody like that? Why did she not pick up the phone and tell me to come over to my grandparent's house? I concluded only a mad woman would have done that. How dare she, I accused. I decided to head over to my grandparent's house. After all I had a bag there I had to pick up. My boyfriend Martin made me stall it out for another hour in his house to cool down my temper and try to pep talk me in to not getting into any arguments when I get there. Of course I agreed.

I entered the house of my grandparents and headed straight up the stairs to where my bag had been sitting in the back room. As soon as I hit the top of the stairs mum was standing there. 'Excuse me' I asked without even looking her in the face so that I could get by without any conflict. But mum was still cussing me and accusing me of saying something to her friend. I brushed past and grabbed my bag and was faced with having to ask for another 'Excuse me' to get by again.

'You see you, you have always been one hell of a handful' she declared. I felt so deeply hurt and offended. Still I tried to say nothing. 'You are nothing but trouble' she blurted out.

Without notice to myself I shouted at the top of my voice 'Bloody hell. I've bloody had enough of this shit. Your boyfriend sexually abused me for years so I don't give a bloody shit about how you bloody feel' Oh my gosh! I had said it. Now here was a second thing I had never done before. I had never sworn at my mum. In my upbringing the words bloody and shit were swear words.

My words caught up with her, a few seconds after I had said it. As if in slow motion, I watched her trying to absorb the information she had just received 'but, but, but' she stammered 'what the hell you a tell me?'

'You heard me' I firmly responded.

'Be Jesus, what me ah hear?' is all she could conjure up to say as she became unsteady, falling against the wall on the middle landing, to support her as she absorbed the information 'You lie!'

Gran ran to mum's aid from behind me and decided to throw me a string of insulting names. So I left and did not return to visit until about three weeks later. Not one person asked me what had happened.

After role-playing out how I would deal with the situation at my counselling session that week and how I would cope with returning back to see the family, I used up a whole packet of pocket-sized tissues when I walked around the corner for my cry that day.

In another role-play I remember having to confront yet another incident that took place with my Gran when I was visiting my mum at the flat I once lived. It was my youngest sister's birthday party. I was standing in the kitchen when unprovoked my Gran started calling me a liar. I asked her why and she began to return a string of hurtful accusations asking me 'Why are you so wicked?' and 'why you go tell lie on your mother about her old boyfriend?' She continued with, 'You're a wicked and evil child.'

I tried my very best to stay calm but her words we're unforgivable and her behaviour became unacceptable when she picked up the walking stick she used and began whipping it across my back when I turned myself on her to walk away. I spun around and grabbed the stick from her hands and declared, 'I will ram this stick down your throat if you ever hit me again.'

My defense made my Gran flip and she began shouting at the top of her voice. 'You're a wicked, wicked, wicked, liar' again and again whilst she attacked me, this time with both hands. Before I could compose and hold her off, my mum rushed into the kitchen and immediately joined in my slaughter with her blows. Both women were cussing and accusing me of being a liar. I began to shout back but their voices where stronger and louder than mine, which resulted in me just crouched down on the floor covering my face whilst screaming and crying.

About ten long seconds later the kitchen door flew open. 'Leave her alone! It happened to me too.'

At that exact moment both women went silent. I realised it was my eldest sibling. Did I just hear right. I'm sure that was what she said. But she never repeated it again and they did not hit me again. Whatever she said, all I could think was 'what, only now am I believed?'

I was so angry with my sister for having kept any kind of information to herself as I believed with this information she could have stopped the verbal and physical abuse I had been subjected to by mum and Gran, along with the accusations and suspicion that I was lying. All I could think was how could she not have come to my aid sooner?

Neville arrived running through the door. 'Hey what going on? I could hear shouting down the road and when I got near to the block of flats, realised it sounded like my family. What's happened?' Neville turned to look at me and from the state of my appearance he immediately realised I had been attacked by the elders. 'Aunt, Gran what have you done to Beverley?' He stepped in to the kitchen and pulled me out and placed me behind his back.

That day, Neville became my hero and saviour. At that moment he made me feel safe because I was emotionally exhausted.

I just turned nineteen when I spoke out about my first experiences of child abuse but I still withheld the names of my other abusers, which followed because of the way they had handled this disclosure.

'No one is to approach any close relative to have sexual relations. I am the LORD.'
The Holy Bible, Leviticus 18:6, New International Version, 1984

Chapter 9:   Piggy in the middle

My counsellor sat through listening to many incidences of incest abuse that was still unfolding in my life with my cousin. She tried to empower me with techniques to help me manage my emotional turmoil towards my cousin for taking my virginity and to address his continuous taking advantage of my vulnerability. But I could never manage to keep to the plan practiced in the counselling room when faced with reality. I simply lacked the courage to speak up. The courage I thought I would have when I needed it did not show its head in my own sanctuary of a bedsit with no one to stop him or protect me from his prowling when I was alone and he came around unexpected and uninvited.

'How's my favourite cousin' he would start in the sweetest of voices.

'I'm fine' I would respond hoping this was just a general conversation we would be having. For some weird reason when he behaved like he was just my cousin, I did not dislike him for what he had been doing.

'You're so beautiful. I wish I could tell the world I love you because you're the perfect woman for me. If I could I would definitely marry you' he would keep repeating this whilst he walked around my standing body with his fingers circling the touch of my flinching body in spiral motions until he stopped in front of me with his fingers having found the outline of my mouth. He began to circle my mouth and I flinched again and stepped backwards to release myself from his touch.

'Don't. Please Neville'

But Neville took the step forward and re-joined his touching of his fingers to my lips. 'You know I love you don't you? Damn your hot Bev.'

'Stop this please Neville.' But his fingers slipped into my mouth and his other hand clasped behind my head and he swiftly stepped in further to embrace me with both his arms and hands putting me into a gently but firm hug-lock and then stuck his tongue directly into my mouth and began twirling it around. I tried pushing him away but I felt locked in. Neville began passionately kissing my face and down my neck and then back up again to my face. 'Neville please don't. I don't want this. Stop it. You're my cousin. Please don't. Neville please!'

But Neville wasn't listening. One of his hands flew up my dress and began tugging at my panties. 'Please Neville, don't.'

'I can't help wanting you Bev. I love you so much. We should never have been cousins.'

Neville lifted one of my legs and I lost balance as I felt him push me down backwards on the bed and fall directly on top of me whilst he continued engulfing my body with his slimy wet kisses.

'Please Neville.' I could not match his strength and found myself loosing the fight to have him removed from off me. So I simply let go the fight and laid there and said nothing more. Neville moved around my entire body kissing, biting and licking it. His fingers began invading my privates and my legs began to gather a little strength to try and lock him off.

'Relax Bev. Enjoy it. I promise I would never hurt you.'

I had a love-hate relationship when he always said that to me. Of course I wanted my big cousin to stand up for me, which he always did in the family conflicts but he failed to see that he was hurting me with what he was doing. My emotions about my cousin were confusing me. He always spoke gently and lovingly to me, yet did what he did.

Neville used to visit frequently now that he lived around the corner. Most times he was just my visiting cousin and then there were times he would go back to reminding me of our special relationship and how special I was. He reminded me that he was there to protect me. He always said that like he meant it. I couldn't find the stop words deep inside of me that I had often empowered the young people whom I worked with.

I had become really close friends with Neville's girlfriend Madeline whom I liked very dearly and always had a great time with her when we hung out. In my heart I wanted to tell her but I thought she might think I was trying to make up a story to break them up because she totally adored everything about him and spoke continuously about wanting to change her surname by legal depol to be recognised as his partner until they could afford to save up to get married and get their own place. Madeline and I spent many nights sleeping in each other's homes. She lived with her mum, sisters and baby brother. These were always fabulous nights and she was fabulous company. We spoke about everything, accept what Neville had ever done to me.

One night as Madeline decided to stay at the bedsit with me for the night, Neville decided he would too. We stayed up having a laugh until it was time to turn the lights off and get some sleep. This took a further ten minutes to achieve as Madeline and I, as usual began making silly noises until a laughter spell would take over us. She was always fun to be around and I loved her company and friendship dearly. This particular night Neville decided to sleep in the middle and I remember him facing his girlfriend and hugging her as I turned my back on them and everyone fell off to sleep.

During the night I was awoken by Neville's hand pulling down my panty. Within the few seconds of waking, I did not and could not move as I panicked to try and recall who was in the bed with me. I remembered that Neville was also in the bed with Madeline. 'Oh my God' is all I could think. I totally refused to move. Neville anchored my panty below my bottom and then began fidgeting as he lay between us. I laid there facing the wall trying to work out what he was doing but refused to move even a muscle. I wondered for a second if he was masturbating. Then I felt him begin to move closer. Just as he moved Madeline sat up and threw the covers off the bed to reveal the evidence to herself as I continued to lay there pretending to sleep on.

'Oh my God, what the hell do you think you're doing Neville?' she shouted. Her voice was trembling and in shock. Still I pretended to sleep on.

'Uhmm, I don't know?' He lied as he shuffled about. I believe he was adjusting his clothes on his exposed manhood. She was not stupid and was not having it. I heard her punch him. 'I'm sorry I don't know what I was doing,' he tried to slime out of this situation.

'You fucking liar Neville. You pulled her knickers down. I could feel you playing with yourself and you were just about to have sex with your own fucking cousin. You sick sick sick bastard!'

I could hear Madeline grabbing her clothes and bag and leave the room cursing and crying, with him chasing close behind her with his clothes. I heard them arguing in my communal kitchen for a while then she returned to the room and said 'Beverley wake up.' I had already pulled the sheet up, so I thought it was obvious I had woken up while they we're out of the room. I turned to face her as she asked, 'why did you let Neville pull your panties down?'

'I didn't, I was sleeping.'

Neville stepped back into the room and they both continued arguing. She accused him of being a pervert and he simply kept saying, 'Mad's, I thought you were sleeping on that side of the bed, I simply must have gotten disorientated'. He even attempted to defend how he was moving about in the bed as being, 'I was trying not to wake Bev up when I was trying to snug up to you, to make love to you' or something like that crap.

All I could think is 'thank you God for protecting me and exposing him,' although I didn't expect it to be in such an embarrassing way for me. However Neville's abuse on me finally ceased from that day.

I've always felt guilty and sad about what happened with Madeline because she truly is my friend and I love her dearly to this very day. I disliked what Neville did to her but I secretly disliked him more for what he had been doing to me. They managed to stay together for several more years.

The day came when I knew I had to tell my counsellor that I no longer needed the sessions. So I did, even though the pains and memories of the past never disappeared.

I was nearly twenty years old.

Maturity

From the Latin, meaning ripeness, the state of adulthood, of completed growth, of full functioning; the end of the process of maturation. The term is widely used, generally with an adjective prefixed to specify the kind of growth achieved; e.g., sexual intellectual maturity, emotional maturity, etc. Note while some of these can be reasonably well defined, such as sexual maturity, most cannot. They are generally value judgements made of a person to reflect how successfully they correspond to socially and culturally accepted norms. What is considered emotionally childish in one society may very well be an aspect of emotional maturity in another
The Penguin Dictionary of Psychology, Second Edition, Arthur S. Reber, Penguin Books, 1985, 1995, London, Page 439

Chapter 10:   The hand that rocks the cradle...

The year I turned twenty, my relationship with my boyfriend Martin had already developed several cracks. My boyfriend had been caught having a love affair with one of our mutual friends. I was certainly hurt and wounded. He had defiled and abused my trust. Healing from the affair was hard, as the trust was never restored, as much as I tried to work on it. It was practically impossible as the other person lived locally and happened to be a sister of one of his brother's girlfriends. Inside my heart simply ached.

I had been holding down five part time jobs across two local boroughs which totalled between forty to fifty hours a week as a youth worker-in-charge of youth groups and as a temporary care worker in children's homes. I often worked between the hours of ten in the morning to ten at night, with occasional sleep-over or waking-night staff shifts at the children's homes and I would still drive over to pick Martin up from his mum's house, where he shared his childhood bedroom with his brother Gerald, then drive us back to mine if we didn't spend the day or night at his. I was continuously considerate when it came to putting in the effort with my boyfriend. He had his own issues that were unlike the favouritism issues I had grown up with in regards to eldest and youngest siblings. His issues were always focused on him being the youngest in his large family.

A couple of months later I travelled to work in the USA for three and a half months. There I enjoyed a sweep-me-off-my-feet-holiday-love-affair. This would result in this lovely sergeant asking me to marry him when he followed me to the airport to see me off on my farewell departure. I couldn't say yes. I so wanted to. I was already in a relationship and regardless how dysfunctional it was, I needed to sort that out. Plus, what would I have told my family. The thought alone was enough for me to let go of this being my destiny.

A year and a half on, whilst I was working at one of the youth clubs in Fulham, one of the young women who was either sixteen or seventeen arrived in the centre in floods of tears accompanied by her friends. I managed to get the attention of one of the friends and asked her what the problem was. It turned out that this young woman had just discovered she was pregnant. I interceded amongst the friends who were somewhat crowding her and asked her if she would like to come with me to the next room. She obliged and I led her with my hug to an empty and more comfortable room. I began by reassuring her that I would not share the information she gave me to anyone unless it was necessary for her own safety. This appeared to instantly put her at ease. I asked her what the problem was and after many gulps for air she revealed she was pregnant.

I then began a series of questioning so I could gather a picture of the situation she now found herself in. I asked her if she had just found out and what was going through her mind at that moment. She revealed her fears were to tell her parents but had already made up her mind that she would be keeping the baby. I then asked if the young man she had been seeing knew she was pregnant and she said he didn't yet. I asked if she knew him well and she responded that she did. I asked if she felt comfortable in telling him and she shrugged her shoulders. I asked if he lived in the same Borough and if he was a local as there were four of the five youth centres that I worked at in the same Borough, it was possible that I too knew this young man and he too would need help and reassurance when he was ready but that was not a concern right at that moment. I asked if we could give the father-to-be a name so I didn't have to keep calling him 'this young man'. She willing shared this as Martin. This of course was a common name, but still my heart and spirit felt like it skipped a jump, sank and then became weary.

Some weeks later I noticed my relationship with my partner became frustratingly difficult more than usual. I suddenly believed he was again having an affair so decided to go through his small, slim black telephone book which he kept in the inside pocket of his jacket. I had done this several times since the last affair. On this occasion I found one of the numbers severely crossed out with lots of scribble and re-enforced loops and swirls as if to disguise what had been there before. As he slept, I decided to hold the page in the book up to the little fluorescent light over the sink in the new bedsit I had moved into about thirteen months earlier. To my surprise I was clearly able to see the name Jilly but couldn't quite make out the numbers. I decided to place my finger on the back of the paper and see if I could work out each number by running my finger over it, as if it were Braille. I managed to gather three possible sets of telephone numbers and returned the phone book back to its pocket in the jacket and took myself back into bed where he laid. That was a long night. I laid there praying and wishing that what I had to ask him wasn't going to be true. The problem I knew I had was admitting later where I got the details from just in case I needed to go back to it again.

In the morning just as we awoke I took my chances. 'Babes?'

'What's up' he asked stretching out any remaining sleep that remained in his body.

'You were tossing and turning nuff last night and then you started speaking in your sleep.' It sounded convincing.

'For real?'

'Yes, for real' I confirmed.

'What was I saying?' I totally had his attention. He was intrigued and I could see he was thinking hard. Probably trying to remember what he was dreaming about.

'You said Jilly you can't have it. You kept saying that like you were in a conversation and you sounded like you were begging and repeated it over again and again.' His face looked like he was in shock. The name as far as I was concerned was an issue.

'Did I say anything else?' He sounded nervous like he was digging for more information, so I gave him more. I knew I had hit the right nail.

'Yes'

'What?'

If it weren't true why would he ask for more information, I thought. 'You said, Jilly you don't know what you've done to me. You can't have it' I stared hard at him and asked 'who's Jilly Martin? What can't she have?' His face told me he was about to lie. 'Don't play with me Martin. Is this Jilly pregnant with your child?'

'I don't know any Jilly and no one is pregnant with my child'. You lying bastard is all I could think.

Later that day after I had dropped Martin back to his home, I decided to call the numbers from a payphone near to his house. 'Please God, please will you declare me the truth' I prayed as I dialled the first of the three numbers and it began to ring. On about its fourth ring the phone was picked up. 'Hello' the voice was definitely that of a young person.

'Hello, can I speak with Jilly please' I tried to sound upbeat and unthreatening although my heart was pounding so hard and my armpits began to perspire.

'Speaking' the voice confirmed.

Oh-my- gosh I told myself. It's the person I'm looking for. 'Hi Jilly, you don't know me. But I had to give you a call. I'm Martin's girlfriend and I'm aware of your pregnancy. I haven't called to make trouble. However I need to make a decision about my five and half-year relationship and I would really appreciate just a few minutes of your time to meet me. We can meet in a public place for a talk.' There was a long silence so I butted in again. 'You are not in any threat or danger from me. I'd like to meet you so you can let me know what you plan to do. It really will help me decide what I'm going to do with my relationship.'

'Ok, where?' she responded. All I could think was 'thank you God'.

'How about in the square near where Go-Gay the drycleaners is? Do you know the one on Wandsworth Bridge Road? There's a park bench there. Do you know where I mean?' Of course she did. It was only a block away from Martin's house and she lived a good ten to fifteen minutes walk away.

'Yes, I know where it is. What time?'

'Can you meet me there in about twenty or thirty minutes?'

There were a couple seconds silence but it felt longer. 'Yes I can' she confirmed.

As I placed down the phone, I realised I was actually feeling ridiculously nervous. I began praying in my head asking God how I was going to manage this one. This was a young woman attending the centre I managed. Plus this was a young woman who attended my girls night sessions at the centre. This was such an uncomfortable situation and that could be perceived very differently if this meeting did not go well or if my line manager or her parents knew that I was the partner of the man who got their daughter pregnant. I seriously began to wonder if this was going to affect my job or worse still if her parents felt a need to report this to someone. I pondered on the age difference that I worked out had to be between three to six years difference. I couldn't remember if she was sixteen or seventeen and if she was seventeen when she would be turning eighteen. The thought of it made me feel sick and sad, all at the same time. My mind began doing overtime. Martin had really pissed me off this time.

 Those thirty minutes took forever. I had made my way down to the square and crossed over to the other side of the road so that I could see her coming. Exactly to the thirty minutes Jilly arrived at the zebra crossing. 'Hey Jilly, how you doing hun? We haven't seen you at girl's night at the youth club for a for a while.'

'Yeah I know' she replied.

'Where are you off too?' I tried to sound like the upbeat inquisitive youth worker.

'Just off to meet someone' she responded.

'I know Jilly, it's me.' Her mouth opened and her jaw looked as if it fell on the floor. 'Come on let's sit and chat.'

That was so hard. I was torn between treating this young woman who I had worked with for some two or three years with respect knowing that I had given my oath to a confidentiality agreement I had earlier offered her. I knew I could do nothing about this sensitive situation. I was torn between being cheated on and the situation of this young and possibly, frightened woman. I released at that moment I was insignificant, again.

My relationship ended less than three weeks later when the pain and resentment became too much to bear. Added to the hurt, the disrespect and insensitive attitude of Martin's mother I endured blew me away. I arrived at their house one day to find a cot had been placed in Martin's bedroom. When she heard me asking Martin why he was rubbing it in my face; his mum flew down the stairs and said to me, 'mind your own business and don't ever let me hear you asking about anything that comes into my house again.' She didn't stop there. She continued with 'remember how you killed off your child for my son when you were sixteen or seventeen.' That was so cold. I had an abortion because I was so frightened at the thought of my family finding fault with me and fulfilling their negative expectations of me. Worse I thought, I was young and unmarried and that would have gone against my own beliefs and values. There was certainly no way I was going to bring children into the world without being married. More so, I had only been convinced by ninety-five to ninety-nine percent that that child would have been his. The remaining percentage laid in doubt with fears that it could had been my cousin's who had been sexually abusing me back then and I could never had taken that chance. Little did they know that in fact I had two abortions for this same reason even though I was on the pill but I kept taking it at adhoc times simply due to my working patterns and being forgetful.

That day was my last day in Martin's house and in his life. I simply walked away when I realised the hurtful truth that no one was going to be fighting my corner on my behalf and I had no control in making right the situation I found myself in. I was now aged twenty-one and a half years of age.

Although mental health problems are very common – affecting around one in four people in Britain – stigma and discrimination towards people with mental health problems is still very common and there are a lot of myths about what different diagnoses mean.

There is also a lot of controversy about the way mental health problems are diagnosed, what causes them, and which treatments are most effective.

However, despite these challenges, it is possible to recover from a mental health problem and live a productive and fulfilling life. It is important to remember that having a mental health problem is not a sign of weakness

Understanding mental health problems, http://www.mind.org.uk/assets/0001/7308/Understanding_mental_health_problems_2011.pdf

Chapter 11:   Shadow of death

Again I sunk to the depths of my lows. I began to feel depressed, lonely, hurt, and angry. I felt totally rejected and unloved and there was no one to talk to about it. As my smoking increased, so did my asthma attacks. I was more annoyed with myself than I was angry with Martin. I felt his lack of honesty and faithfulness was below the line but I had to be honest and agree with myself that we had outgrown each other anyway. Merely because Martin did not have any drive or zest for life or at least sparks of confidence within him. As much as I had grown to love that family, I had to look at his other five siblings who all had children with their long-term partners, but none were married or lived away from home really. They stayed at their partner's houses but every little fall out they were there, back in their childhood home and childhood bedrooms. I realised that this was not the path for me. Martin did not pertain to have the independence or emotional stability I needed in my life and in a partner. He had never been able to support me as I tried to find my way through my own emotional turns that often filled me with tears. He was never able to fill such sensitive moments with empowering words or support. Instead he would just add to my burdens and troubles.

Over the coming year my memories of my childhood had become unbearable to live with. I kept getting flash backs from my first experience I had of being abused by Terry. The flashbacks kept replaying my choking on his penis and not being able to breathe. I remembered the confusion and fear I felt at not knowing what was happening or why. Then there were thoughts of no-one coming to rescue me from the years of my abuse as a child from one situation to another. All this kept rolling around in my head. I was still holding on to so much pain having only exposed just one of my long kept secrets about one of my abusers in that heated confrontation with my mum. I found myself trying to reassure myself that if my interfering grandmother had not got involved that day I accidentally spouted it out, then my mum's reactions might had been different. Some of us grandchildren found our grandmother to be quite a spiteful woman when she was ready. She bore no shame in highlighting which children she refused to adopt as her favourites and I for sure definitely wasn't one of them. I wondered if my mum would have been able to sit me down properly and ask me what happened instead of the silent treatment I now experienced as if I had never spoken those words. Ever. Instead no one asked. Only my Gran chose to speak about it whenever she felt the urge. Sadly for me, the only words she could find to say was 'You liar!' I felt more isolated and lonely now than ever before when no one knew except my best friend, who died with my secret.

Somehow I managed to keep my emotions hidden and self-contained by my continued effort to fill my worth with my working life and making sure it was abundantly filled from the time I woke till night. From the age of fifteen I had developed a burning desire and passion to protect the lives of other vulnerable young people and women and this orchestrated my vision. This I believed is why I had been put here on this earth and something I knew I would always believe in. Even if I didn't have the courage to face my own hurts, I was certainly motivated to help others.

I strongly felt that young people and vulnerably adults needed to be reassured that they didn't have to settle with being in situations that they were not comfortable with, even if life predicted it for them. They needed to be encouraged to embrace their own personal choices and the courage to dig down deep and pull up the confidence that is laying there within them covered in fear, shame, neglect and so many more obstacles just needing to break through and come up and out. They needed someone to help them to find or create opportunities that would give them back the special and inspiring things that would help them create the visions they desired for their own lives. I believed vulnerably people, especially the young were worth it for they were the special ones on this earth and I strongly believe they have so much to offer which might ultimately help or save the life of another person in times to come.

I loved working but I also needed to, as I had bills to pay. I kept opting to take on more sessions at the youth clubs so that I could dedicate myself to vulnerably young people. I was now involved in girls and women's groups, doing generic youth works sessions, unemployment projects and street based work to engage with people who didn't use mainstream services. My ability to engage and motivate people to explore sensitive issues by using group work discussions and motivational resources simply helped to get them to think about their choices, their decisions, their attitudes, their values and their rights. I was able to nurture their thoughts on personal management, cultural issues, emotional issues and relationships choices, and addictions to even exploring and addressing abuse in their lives.

It was during one of my sessions at a youth club in Fulham, that I became in regular contact with Trevor who was the deputy youth worker. I had seen him and heard his name around the work circuit. Most being positive and some being gossip about him hanging with most of the people I grew up with and who he was suppose to be dating. However I didn't know him personally. One day Trevor approached me in the office and told me about the counselling service that he was opening up for young people now that he had obtained his counselling degree. He asked me if I wanted to encourage some of the young people to take up the sessions. This I knew I could do as I had a natural rapport with them that enabled them to engage and talk easily. Trevor said he could see in my eyes that there were deep-rooted issues that were troubling me. I tried to brush off his comments but his empathic way about him seemed quiet nurturing. He prodded on with a few more of those probing questions that touched the root of my soul and I surprised myself when a tear from one of my eyes trickled out to expose me as a liar and hiding the truth.

Trevor encouraged me to come along to see him on about six occasions for his counselling service in the afternoons when the club sessions were not in progress. I guessed that way I didn't have to feel like I was being exposed to my colleagues or the young people themselves. We could use the cover of a meeting if anyone was to see me. These were uplifting sessions. First three were of course the painful ones, telling it all and the other three suddenly moved into getting me to see how fantastic I was and skillful in my work. He began exploring my current plans for studying to qualify as a full-time youth and community worker to top up the qualifications I already had, which I had already begun applying to universities to do.

Trevor and I had nothing other than the work we did in common. I was no way attracted to him. The man had teeth like a street of burnt out houses. He was slimmer than me. But he was indeed very sociable and had a calm, charming and gentle approach to everything. My youngest sister attended the youth club and knew Trevor more than I did and so did most of the people working in the club. Somehow my youngest sister made reference to coming up to my flat where I was now living in Streatham which somehow he got invited to. From there, Trevor somehow kept coming back every night for about a week as my flat was always filled with family relatives coming over.

My family always generated jokes and laughter every time we came together. I had spent the last six or so years hanging out with my slightly younger brother and my eldest sister. We shared the same circle of friends, threw annual parties and were there for each other. My youngest sister was always around me too as she also lived by herself and was a bus ride away. I can't think of a dull moment with my family throughout my whole life. Because of the energy we excel we attracted many people and their families into our ever-growing family cell.

Trevor enjoyed those evenings. I could tell. All the silly and mischievous games we got up to as a family and as adults were simply too funny. Like, True, Dare, Double, Dare. I remember sending one of our family friends to sit cross-legged in the middle of my communal car park that was over looked by all the surrounding blocks and a nearby hostel. They were made to eat my Caribbean cooked rice and peas from one of the big catering pots I had, with music playing and blaring out next to them. Some of the ideas were of course simply foolish but no one wanted the forfeit and everyone knew it was better to take the task and not the punishment. I decided to take the punishment one day as my True, Dare, Double, Dare task was to kiss Trevor. They were crazy! No way! My forfeit was to fill a spoon with Caribbean hot pepper sauce and hold it in my mouth for two minutes. I suffered with swollen lips that day.

Trevor invited me to go for a drive down to Brighton Pier one evening during the week. That sounded like such fun, and it was. Brighton is a beautiful place. A little similar to London but the added pier and seashore provided fun activities alongside the mindful stroll which the rivers in London did not do for me. I enjoyed the company. As we were sitting on the pebbled beach, Trevor asked me if I'd like to go out with him as his girlfriend. I had to admit to myself; having had those counselling sessions with him I was left feeling slightly attached to him emotionally. No one had ever listened to me the way he had and I felt a genuine closeness to him because of it. I did not find him attractive but this wasn't an issue for me.

Over the next two years Trevor and I had developed our future plans and I was to be his wife. We took my mum and her new partner who actually turned out to have been my mum's first childhood love; out for a meal and Trevor asked for their permission to marry me. Then followed the announcement to all my family in a special dinner gathering in what was now our flat and then came the bridal arrangements and purchasing for our big day. Up until this point I was the most loved up woman in the world. I was the most happiest and troubled free than I had ever experienced possible. Trevor did not have any past baggage or a connection that comes with living life. He had no links with his biological family or past associations. He said he stopped talking to his mum and dad who were also from Barbados, when he was just sixteen and had not seen them in sixteen years. He said the only thing he had to do was pay off for something that he and his ex girlfriend took out when they were living together but that would be cleared in a couple of years. I just assumed it was repayment on furniture.

The bridal dates for the registry office were confirmed and we knew the date we needed to return on to secure the date of the booking we wanted. We had sorted our wedding reception at one of my relative's house for a garden wedding; the menu was agreed and Trevor paid for my bridal dress which was in an African print for a traditional African themed celebration after the registry office and our cutlery and crockery were ordered from the States, to co-ordinate with my dress and our theme.

During this time I decided to kill two birds with one stone and pop into my local Well Woman Clinic for a general check up as I was on my way to my first Tia-chi competition that I had been so very much excited about having trained really hard for the past thirteen months. On examination at the clinic, I discovered I was pregnant. I was so excited. Although Trevor and I had said we wanted children as soon as we married, I thought it was going to take me a while to conceive so got Trevor to agree that it was ok for me to come off the contraceptive pills I had been taking. Hearing I was pregnant was wonderful. At least I would be married before I gave birth, as Trevor understood my importance of never wanting to be a single parent. Just my mum had raised me after the breakup of her marriage to dad. I was adamant from a really young age that I wanted both parents for my children and throughout their lives.

Trevor seemed to receive the news with great happiness and so thereafter he increased his working hours so he could increase his finances and added in private counselling work. He also upped his volunteering hours for some support phone lines he helped out with and spoke about the supervision sessions with his counselling supervisor for the cases he was currently managing. His time at home was almost non-existent. All of a sudden he also had tons of weekends away with young people he said he had to fulfill to make up the post-qualification he said were attached to the child abuse training he did. Our paths seemed to cross over nearing midnight several times a week. My days were now filled with studying for my youth and community work full time course and then rushing to do my evening work at some of the youth centres I kept contracts with. As I no longer worked at the youth club Trevor was based at so I would call him if I missed him in the mornings to check what his programme for the day entailed and be able to touch base with him.

When Trevor was in, we had an explosive and exciting sex life but he wasn't talking anymore. For some unknown reason, I went to bed one night and asked 'are you having an affair?' I was now 3 months pregnant and we were due to be married in less than five months time. I guess in that moment of time my spirit must have alerted itself because this thought had never before crossed my mind.

'That's it; I've had enough of your questions. We're done' was his one and only response to my one and only question.

I couldn't believe the words I just heard. How can you finish with me because I asked that question? How could you not want to discuss it? Who is this person that you're seeing that you could want to throw away our future like it was nothing? But we're due to be married in a few months? Our flat is full of bridal purchases, how can you say that and I am pregnant? I watched him turn his back and pull the covers up over his head. He just went cold on me refusing to answer anything I asked. I decided this was not over but I knew tonight I would not find any of the answers I needed to make sense of this. He was my saviour. I had placed him on the pedestal I had created for him. Why would he now say this? This was a long night and a short morning. He left for work without talking to me or having breakfast.

I was running a summer programme at one of the centres I worked at. I arrived to work looking like I was in shock, as much as I tried to hide it, it was truly very difficult. After discussing what had happened with my colleague she encouraged me to take the time out of the session and to return at the end to lock up. I sat in my car and spent the next few minutes thinking. Who are Trevor's friends? He only had a few he spoke about and only one who lived near me I knew where he lived. But there was this one particular street where I had often seen his car parked on and when I always mentioned it, he would always respond with, 'I was in a committee meeting on that road' or 'I was visiting my friend Elise and my God-daughter. I decided to head down there to try work out where exactly Elise lived.

I knocked on each door and gave the description of a black woman with a little girl until I was pointed in the right direction. I rang the doorbell and could swear I saw the curtains move but no one came down. I returned to work and stayed for another hour and then headed back to the flat with the twitching curtain. I was persistent in my ringing of the bell. Then the door opened and there stood a woman. 'Are you Elise?'

'Yes' she responded still holding on to the door so that it disclosed only half of her body.

'Are you and Trevor having an affair?' Whatever made me ask that? I was meant to ask if she had a child and the Godfather is Trevor.

'You'd better ask him that' and with that she closed the door. I stood there for a few more seconds and saw the curtains twitch again.

Did I hear her right? I jumped into my car and sped over to Trevor's youth club. Just as I was parking the car I noticed Trevor run out of the club and jump into his car. I followed him. He took me back to the house I had just come from and he walked over and put a key in the door

'You bastard' I screamed at him.

He turned and walked back towards me. 'I want out of your life. I want nothing to do with you. Don't you dare come around here! That's it I'm packing' he threatened and without any opportunity to discuss anything he jumped back into his car and sped off.

We seemed to be racing all the way back to our flat. Trevor was way ahead with his sports engine. When I arrived home twenty-five minutes after we set off he had already packed all his clothes into big black bin liners and was working on detaching his computer. 'Hold on a minute, how can you just walk out like this? If you've got some issues how can you respond like this? We're supposed to be getting married? For Christ sake I'm carrying your baby.' He did not respond, just continued packing up his belongings into his car. He was all packed up in what seemed like five minutes after my arrival home and then he was gone. I was truly numb. I couldn't work out if what just happened truly did happen.

Another interaction with Elise two days later sealed my mental breakdown for the duration of my pregnancy. She told me Trevor said I was a mad woman who he only slept with once and thereafter I'd been stalking him. That hurt so much. The next week I attempted suicide twice with an overdose cocktail of old prescription tablets. Both times I had my door kicked in or opened by suspicious and loving friends and family who feared that to be my outcome. On both occasions I awoke in hospital. On the second occasion I could hear one of my aunt's close friends who had known me all my life, talking with a doctor. It seemed that they were talking about sectioning me under the mental health act or something. She seemed to be negotiating on my behalf saying that I was a jilted bride-to-be who was pregnant and needed someone to talk to and not sectioning. It was then agreed that I would have to attend a psychological assessment and therapy in a mental health centre on a daily basis as an outpatient. I did this daily for about three months or so until it was agreed I was going through a bereavement process for the loss I had encountered.

I was also under observation from now on by my family. This alone with the daily sessions with the psychiatrist made me realise I had to take control of my life. I had to give my unborn child a better start. I had to be whole for him or her. I endured a lonely pregnancy and a hard one too. But I got there.

Trevor knocked the front door six weeks after I gave birth. I was so furious I made my youngest sister tell him I could not see him. Over the years I saw him once in court for child maintenance payments and another time in a nightclub. But put that aside, the first time he met his daughter she was already eight years old.

At the time of my pregnancy I was twenty-five years old.

In Women's Aid's view domestic violence is physical, sexual, psychological or financial violence which takes place within an intimate or family-type relationship and that forms pattern of coercive and controlling behaviour'

Women's Aid, Domestic Violence: Frequently Asked Questions Factsheet 2009

Chapter 12:   For the love of God

Three weeks after the birth of my daughter, I met this guy named Danny at a friend's party. Over the coming months at the repeat party scene he'd arrive around the same 3am time. He was a musician, so after doing his thing would hit the party scene. It became a habit of his to look out for me and suddenly I felt alive again. After all, someone was taking an interest in me and that felt nice. We had so far only seen each other at nights and we hadn't really had a proper conversation but I could feel this really strong energy connection that was flowing between us, which made me feel alert, aware and noticed. When we danced, I felt light headed. Somehow the gentle but firm way that he held me made me feel like I was being protected. There was differently an attraction thing going on.

One day I decided to buck up the courage and invite Danny over to my house for lunch. I was really looking forward to meeting and seeing who the real Danny was. He arrived about forty minutes later than I had confirmed with a big friendly smile on his face, which threw me off from seeking an apology for his lateness. I guess I was simply pleased he had showed up. We appeared to get on relatively well, with most of our conversations ending in laughter and Danny appeared to be really attentive. He followed me to the kitchen and amazed me with his helpfulness. He helped me finish laying the table and then transferred the cooked food into serving plates and placed them on to the table. During our lunch I excused myself from the table to attend to breast feed my waking daughter in the privacy of my bedroom and returned with her fed and nappy changed to find he had placed my plate of food in a warm oven. After lunch, without asking he washed the dishes and then took the kitchen trash and dirty nappies sealed in their scented bags to the rubbish bins outside. Something so simple somehow made me like him more.

Danny told me he was a full-time musician and spent his days recording music and his evening performing in nightclubs and other venues. His was a totally different world to mine. Lunchtime turned into an evening meal and talking the whole day away until almost mid night. Danny asked if we could get together again as he really enjoyed my company. That for me was simply such a lovely and warming thing to hear. It actually felt nice after the year I had just gone through with being abandoned by my fiancée who was the father of my child and going through the last two suicide attempts. Somehow Danny's charming company made me feel special again so I invited him back to visit me in my home the following week. On that occasion he made his interest known in wanting to pursue a relationship with my daughter and me.

As we were nearing towards three months of the relationship I became tired of his routines, which I somehow found I had begun accommodating. I found Danny to be someone who would willingly and happily take from someone but not truly contribute. Being on a maternity leave and pay, it was quickly becoming apparent that I could not carry the daily expense of feeding this man and allowing him to drive up the cost of my utility bills to a soaring amount that I was ill-prepared for. He simply did not have a giving nature about him. He had never brought food into the house yet took over most of the cooking of the meals. He never even brought my daughter a baby biscuit as a suggestive gift but had the cheek whenever he accompanied me on my weekly shopping trips to add things in the trolley and stack them on the conveyor belt but yet did not put his hand in his pocket to pull out any cash when it came to paying for it. I made sure I nipped that in the bud and told him I had a strict budget so he'd have to pay for the things he wanted. That stopped him putting things in the shopping trolley. The man was tight. He was great with my daughter and had no objection to changing the smelliest of nappies; making her food or settling her down.

Danny had managed to slowly move in some of his clothes and began helping me to wash my clothes whilst adding in a few garments of his own, whilst he was at it. He was there eating me out of house and home, on a daily basis so I decided to end it. My attempts to finish the relationship did not go the way I had expected it. Danny refused to accept it as ended. He shouted. Then he threatened me for having the disgusting thoughts of taking apart what he believed God had put together. With that he punched the wall in the hallway right next to my left ear, leaving the indentation of all his knuckles embedded as an outline. I was so petrified I froze yet I could hear my heart racing in my chest and ear. He immediately switched to shower me with hugs and kisses. I knew I was out of my depths and I was so frightened. My daughter's crying broke his release of me to go and warm her bottle for her feed. I vowed after the first indent, never to cover that up with decorating plaster until the relationship ended. I knew that at least that way I could never forget about the type of man this was and what he might be capable of.

By the first year I lost count at the amount of times I attempted to end this dysfunctional relationship. I got to seven then stopped counting. His temper was to terrifying. Each time I endured threats and accusations. He would either hover over me for long periods with a puffed up chest dictating to me what I should be doing to contribute to our family instead of breaking it up whilst starring hard at me. This man had taken claim that my family was his and belonged to him and I did not know how to take it back. After his tantrums he would always speak to me in a soft voice and tell me to let him know how much I loved

122

him. The problem with this was always his tactic once he pinned me in a corner unable to move.

At least five of these seven times I told him we were finished and I did not want to be in the relationship he stormed off to go pack the bags he had brought into my home without my invitation. Whilst he packed I would always hear him cussing out aloud swapping his British sounding accent to that of his Jamaican-born one and asking himself 'seh how she fi do mi so?' However the performance went, he simply would never just leave. He would get to the front door and throw a string of accusations about how selfish I was and how fond he was of me and my daughter, which he treated as his own. Once those bags left his hand to drop to the floor I was always ensured that this would follow a minimum of 2hrs twisting around all my responses until I'd became exhausted in responding. Then he would move in for the kill by dosing me with endless hugs, kisses and telling me not to be so hasty with throwing away such a good thing.

I realised I was in a relationship I felt stuck in. I also felt a huge sense of embarrassment that I had a very professional career working with vulnerably children and adults and building their self esteem and confidence yet I was living in fear in my home unable to stand up to my very own bully. Amazingly, his temper only ever showed its head when I tried to end the relationship. Outside of that he kept trying to charm me. Most of the times his inability to be a provider or contributor simply annoyed me, even if he looked busy cooking, cleaning and helping in the household.

I tried again five years later and he did finally walk out the door after hours of cursing what he considered was a foolish decision I was making and after more indents in walls and of course cornering me like I was his prey, he did leave.

Immediately I had one of my brother change the locks on the front door so that Danny could not return and use what once used to be my spare set of keys that he still possessed. Not having him around almost made me more nervous than him being there. My spirit was uneasy, as I believed he was not going to allow this to be a final decision in our chapter. Whenever I saw a car that looked like his my heart would pound and my hands become clammy. All of a sudden, I would notice his look-a-like cars everywhere. I was so on edge and mentally feeling stressed and nervous. It wasn't long before I knew I would be right. By the third evening my house phone and mobile received messages on their answer phones every few hours which soon increased to every hour during the week days evenings and randomly at the weekend as he probably accepted I was visiting my mum's house so would not be picking up the messages until Monday anyway. The first time I played the house messages my daughter heard his voice and burst out in tears, telling me that I was stopping her from being with this man whom she referred to as daddy. At the end of the second week Danny turned up at the front door and I opened it without first looking out of the window to see who it was. He stood there with a child's bicycle in his hand. This was the first of any gift he had ever given to her. He stood there and said 'is Munchie there please?' calling her by the nickname he had given to her since she was a baby.

As soon as my daughter heard her nickname she ran screaming, crying and rejoicing with the words 'Daddy' to the front door. He took forever to hug her and kept looking at me with his blaming eyes which told me that he was thinking I was selfish for breaking up this family and for not giving him children fully knowing that he didn't have any that was biologically his own. 'Daddy are you coming home?'

'Can I come home mummy?'

How dare you start this in front of my child is all I could think. They both stood there starring at me for my answer. I refused to answer and my daughter began pleading his defence with tears and excitement for her gift.

'Daddy teach me how to ride this big bike please? Now please, can I daddy?'

'Of course darling, let's ask mummy and if mummy says yes then you can do it now.' He responded starring at me.

All I could think was 'Oh how you love to play good cop, bad cop but don't think your using my child to get what you want'.

'Please mummy please? Please can I? Please can daddy help me? Please?'

I could clearly see what he was up to but was ill equipped and unprepared to cope emotionally with my daughter's anxieties and questions as she begged for my yes response. 'This is not a good time' I tried to stall on the answer.

'I don't want to watch anymore of that cartoon' she responded. I felt foolish, as it was obvious I was trying to make excuses knowing that I was not doing anything of great importance at the moment. 'Please mummy, please can I?' My heart was aching for my daughter's broken heart. She adored Danny.

'Ok but only for twenty minutes.' I did not trust him and knew I did not want him back inside my home.

'Thank you mummy, I love you.' With those words she turned and hugged me. Part of me hated that response as it was just making this situation and conversation more difficult with Danny and was simply supporting his idea that I was the cause of breaking up this so-called-family-unit and the love that should be found within one.

125

It took Danny about twenty minutes to put the damn stabilisers on her new bike at the front door. Followed by, ten minutes adjusting the seat height in accordance to length of her leg by having her sit on and off the bike. Then Danny insisted on giving a five minutes prep talk to my daughter for her challenge of riding her new and bigger bike to the one I had bought her only a year ago. Just as I thought this charade was over he sent her in the house to go and look for her helmet, leaving me on the doorstep on my own with this manipulator.

'I really appreciate this. I've missed her so much. The last couple weeks have been so hard without you both in my life.'

With perfect timing my daughter ran back to the door with her helmet in hand and a massive smile across her face 'I'm ready daddy'. I so disliked her calling him this.

I did not even utter one word to Danny but I knew he would return after the bike ride to pick up where he had left off. That bicycle ride took another 1hour 29 minutes and 59 seconds until I interrupted it to say she needed to come in for her dinner. On hearing this, my daughter then started pleading for Danny to stay for dinner as well. I felt so awkward.

The evening dragged away and soon it was my daughter's bedtime and then hours passed by and Danny was still wearing me down with endless reasons why he knew we were supposed to be a family unit. When he finally left my home it was nearly four o'clock in the morning and he tried to indicate that he was leaving as a favour knowing that I had to get some sleep as I had work in the morning and would be up in the next three and a half hours.

The next evening, five minutes after arriving home from work the phone rang and it was him telling me that he wanted to pop in to give me something. I declined but he kept insisting that he was now only five minutes away and would give it to me and then will leave me alone to sort myself out as he knew I had probably only just stepped in from work and from picking my daughter up from the child-minders, so knew I would be busy. Straight away I felt myself preparing my defensiveness, as I knew he was simply trying to wear me down. He knew my routine well and there was no way he just happened to be in the local area when he lived fifteen miles away.

Two minutes and a few seconds later the doorbell rang. The glass panel in the door outlined his physique as he stood so close to the door and immediately on looking my daughter shouted, 'it's daddy.'

As I opened the door she ran in front of me and gave him a hug and he hugged her with one arm and the other arm he brought from behind his back and produce a beautiful boutique of flowers saying 'and these are for you because daddy didn't bring mummy a present yesterday.'

'I didn't need you to get me no flowers Danny. I simply want to move on' I refused to raise my hands to even accept them.

'Take them please' he pleaded. But not waiting too long for my answer he gave them to my daughter and asked her to put them inside so that mummy could sort them out.

'Can I come in?' he dared to ask.

'No Danny, I'm tired and I've got a lot of things to do.'

'That's ok, I'll just spend a bit of time with Munchie and then I'll go.' Again my daughter heard him call her name and request to stay and play with her and again I felt like I was being held hostage by her tears and pleas.

'No Danny, I'm totally shattered from last night and I have got too much to do. Please leave now.' I tried ignoring my daughter. I really was too tired and knew I did not have the confidence or energy to even take Danny on from inside my home so knew it was vital to keep him on this side of the door. I had to raise my voice to put my foot firmly down to be heard 'Danny please leave, you know you're just upsetting her being here and you're making this harder and more stressful for me too.' Danny left but came back three more times later that week.

By the third week of interruptions with Danny, I found myself unwillingly back in the relationship simply by duress. It only took a couple of weeks before the real Danny showed his ugly head again because I was unable to hide my dissatisfaction at being back in the relationship, as much as I tried. It bugged me that he was in my home; washing my clothes or preparing my food. I did not give him a replacement spare door key for the new lock on the front door so on several occasions around 3am, Danny would call me on the house phone to wake me up to tell me he was at the front door. My annoyance was noted on some occasions to the disruption and a few nights in the week he chose to return to his mother's house which he had always occupied in Wandsworth whilst she lived her retirement back in Jamaica.

My unwillingness to submit wholeheartedly to the relationship began to cause Danny a degree of upset. He would arrive in a smiley mood and within minutes of not giving him the welcoming response he was looking for from me when he hugged or went to kiss me, his mood would change for the rest of the night. I could feel him starring distastefully at me when I was not looking directly at him. I could hear him closing cupboard doors in the kitchen and allowing them to slam shut. I could hear him cussing under his breath about me too. One day his tolerance levels changed and his muttering became more vocal; his tone more flat; and his actions more abrupt. He persistently followed me around the house telling me how sick I was at not knowing a good thing in my life when I had it. I dismissed his way of thinking. In my own thoughts I could only calculate the financial burden I experienced as I fed this worthless-good-for-nothing-man who lacked the true knowledge of what it was like to truly participated and contribute to family life. He acted as if he was a great catch but this man was a burden and embarrassment. I had never invited him to any public events I attended related to my work and whenever I could avoid it, to any of my family functions too. Although, I would purposely ask him for his help at any of the charitable fundraising holistic health day events I began to run each month because I knew I needed help with transportation and a handyman. Danny would help me set up within the allocated hour or pull down and pack up in thirty minutes. Once he did either end he never stayed longer than he had to anyway.

Danny was rarely available or seen on my return from work so I would take the liberty of reminding him at the very last minute about any parents' evenings knowing he would most often than not say he was unavailable which I always greeted as being a blessing. I was more worried about his clown-like behaviour he couldn't help exhibiting and with his over exemplified and caricature answers and body language as if he had this personal need to be seen, heard and accepted and loved by everyone. If he attended, he would display an over concerned attitude and interest when hearing how much effort my daughter was putting in to her work although she was still working just below that of the national standards for her age. However I knew he had never participated in helping her with her homework which I did routinely everyday with her. He never asked her about her day or read her bedtime books because he was not there when she retired to bed at 8pm and he was always sleeping when she awoke for school again in the morning. So every time I saw his expressions or heard him speak all I could think was 'you're so damn fake'.

His temperament moved on to having physical outbursts and tantrums. He would speak to me from an adjourning room then stamp into my space in a threatening manner and demand an answer from me and accuse me of trying to wind him up. The problem was it was generally between

1am and 3am and more often than not I had fallen asleep on the sofa in front of the television. On some of those occasions he was right, I had laid there pretending to sleep, although I was indeed tired.

On a couple of occasions I had to report him to the police once the wall punching and the intimidation started again. I knew I was out of my depths in this relationship and didn't know where to turn or what to do. I truly started to fear that the only way I was going to finally get out of this relationship was to either immigrate to somewhere in the world by packing and disappearing from my house before he arrived back one morning before 3am or my other possible exit option would be in a coffin.

This triggered my need to be more prepared in planning my next attempted escape from this relationship and this man so that he could not attempt to wear me down again. The preparation for that next time came sooner than I had imagined. Less than a month later, I moved out of my own home and into the home of my best friend Heather, for six weeks after disclosing to her what had been going on the evening before children broke up for their summer holidays. She insisted I get out and come and stay with her the very next day. Heather and her home were my sanctuary. I sent my daughter to my mum's house for the six weeks making it feel like the normal half term holiday plan arrangements without having to tell mum why or expose what had been going on. I actually felt embarrassed and ashamed.

Heather persuaded me to disclose what was happening at home by confiding in my line manager, who was also the Head of Service at the young people's charity I worked at. This actually helped by making me feel even safer for the six weeks of my plan. She moved me to another office in another area and instructed all employees that no one was allowed to give out personal details or information about any staff to the general public and then circulated the related policy to all offices. That was just a general reminder policy and no one else was any the wiser about my situation or problems.

Having now found refuge for myself, I began to reflect on my own life at different times I had become a refuge for two such women. One of which I knew and one that I didn't. The first one I had met when I must have been about seventeen or eighteen years old. I had just come out from watching a midnight movie at the cinema and was walking over Putney Bridge with my sister and her boyfriend Gerald. Just as we reached the bus stop on the same side as the cinema I noticed a women standing on top of the bridge facing towards the river. I nudged my sister and at the same time stopped to speak to the woman.

'Are you ok love?' She did not answer but I could hear her crying. 'Hey hon, whatever it is. It's not worth it. I've been there'. My heart was racing as I absorbed the reality of the moment. Shit, this woman is going to jump.

'Rarse!' I heard Gerald say. I squinted at him as if to imply shut up.

'Please don't do this hon. Please I'm begging you. Talk to me! Please talk to me'.

'I can't take anymore!' I heard her murmur.

'Tell me. What's happened?' She simply stood there with her hair flying in the wind looking straight out into the distance. 'Please come down. Come with me and I will take you home with me for a few days.' I felt my sister nudge me in my side as if to indicate I was being stupid because I didn't know this woman. Knowing my sister she would have been more worried about my safety.

'Please, leave me alone' She said without moving her head to break her distant gaze.

'I'm not going to leave you. Please come home with me. I promise you if you come to my home for the next few days just to give yourself a break from whatever is going on in your life, then I promise you I will let you go without stopping you. But I'm begging you now to allow me to be your friend.' I spoke in the most desperate voice and stayed there begging her relentlessly for the next ten to fifteen minutes until she finally accepted my invitation and I was able to help her down. I could see my sister did not like the idea one bit, but to give her piece of mind I told her I would call her from the payphone in the house I lived in, when I got in.

I linked arms with this woman and took her onto the bus when it pulled up and paid her fare, a few minutes later. I spoke gentle chitchat with her all the way home on that one bus. 'My name is Beverley. I feel so honoured you found me trustworthy. I live in Tooting Broadway in a bedsit and my landlord doesn't live on the premises so no-one will question me as to who you are if you stay a few days.'

'I don't want to be a bother,' she said with evidence of dried eye water and makeup left as tracks down her face.

'I promise you, you're not' I was conscious of making her feel comfortable with me as I had this fear she might change her mind at some point during our journey which I was praying would not take us too long to get home this time of night.

'My name is Sandra'

Sandra and I stayed up all night talking. She told me her horrible story. She had fallen in love with a man who she ended up marrying after a six week love affair to find him turn into an abusive monster the day after their wedding, nearly four years earlier. She said he had made her prostitute herself to clients he had brought to her in the first few months of marriage and since then he drops her off in the red light area of Balham nearly seven days a week and picks her up at the same spot around four or five o'clock every morning. She said he owned everything she had. She had no money, no door key and no access to family or friends since she married him.

Her story made me realise how very fortunate I was not to have fallen into the hands of a pimp from the vulnerably age of sixteen years old living on my own. Worse was the thought of not being able to support my own needs and being forced to live that life as I knew many young and abused women did when they found themselves street homeless.

Sandra spent four nights under the same roof as me but not necessarily in my bedsit. She caught the eye of Victor a Scottish guy who lived one floor directly above mine. I could hear them at it every night. I knew this wasn't helping her but at the same time I was glad she had not jumped. One day when I came home in between my working shifts, I realised she had gone. On my pillow were the simple words, 'thank you' written on a scrap piece of paper with one kiss on. I never saw Sandra again.

On another occasion, I became a place of refuge for a childhood friend who was running away from her childhood sweetheart. Sharon arrived at my door one day with a swollen black eye. Her story was she had finally left Gary but needed a place to stay. I could not refuse her but had to give her some ultimatums about her temporary accommodation. I told her that Gary was never to be allowed in my house and it was only for a few days. It took almost six months to get her to move out but this finally came when she broke the first promise of not letting him in my home. That day, he beat her to a pulp and smashed up her portable television along with stealing my coins from the empty 4.5litre whiskey bottle I had been showcasing my coin savings in the corner of my bedsit. I swore then to myself, that if anyone hit me like that I would kill them. How ironic that statement was now I thought.

133

After the end of the six weeks of refuge in my friend's home, I returned home. Less than one week later, Danny was back in my life and in my house with his worming, accusations of me killing the family and continual harassing me. Again he attempted to use the love of my child as his claim for sharing the parenting although he hardly saw her or even me for that matter as he lived and worked the life of a musician.

During that fifth year of our relationship I discovered he did in fact have three teenage children. I had been seeing them regularly but had not known they were his children as they called him by his stage name. Plus Danny had previously told me they were his sisters' and brothers' children. Then came, the next big lie to unfold when I discovered he had aged from being only four years older than me to being eleven years older. I demanding to see his passport only confirmed this. I could no longer trust his word on anything.

During this same year I was visited in my sleep with a message from God in the most powerful and real like vision, like the one I remembered when I was fourteen. I was instructed to change my name and the name of my child on her fifth birthday. I sincerely believed this did not mean my daughter's first two names as I have received those in my visions as a teenager. Three weeks later as I organised my final preparations to swear an oath in front of two different solicitors and having organised a traditional African naming ceremony as a celebration, I was visited with a vision again during my sleep, over three consecutive nights and I received instructions of my given names which were to be Malakh Evven-Shethiyah Israeel. Even this caused Danny and me conflict as he bullied me into giving up the last name I had received in my vision for a different biblical one. I returned to prayer and reading my Bible for a helping hand forward. The Bible had grown to become both my helper and weapon of protection against this man and it also delivered me much comfort and an internally peaceful feeling, as he did not interrupt me when he saw me reading it. Soon after, I came across the name Zebulun and felt some kind of energy and spiritual connection with it so began praying and asking God for forgiveness of my disobedience to Him and then took that name instead of Israeel.

Nearing six and a half years in the relationship, I also found myself pregnant. I was so worried for my future and that of my current child by making Danny officially and legally part of our family with his very own child. So I aborted the baby. The day after the abortion, I broke down crying and was so full of remorse for the actions I had taken yet again in my life. I spoke with my eldest sister who was so nurturing and understanding. She said 'Malakh if you want a baby, just have one. Don't look and see if he's going to help. You've got your family and you've definitely got me.' She was not aware of the violence but her words made me feel stronger and clearer. Less than six weeks later I was pregnant again.

Danny and I had planned to go to Jamaica for a holiday to his mum's house. Just two months before we were due to travel, I could feel in my bones he was going to flip in his temperament. I left the house as quickly as I could one morning as the tension felt above boiling point and his trigger switches appeared to be getting shorter. I dropped my daughter to school early, as I needed her to be out of the way after I noticed his responses changed from his usual loving mood towards her. Twenty minutes after my return, Danny head butted me and knocked me out flat. I lay there, unconscious and five months pregnant. I recall being revived by the kicks he was giving me in the side of my rib cage, as I laid there. Again he accused me of breaking up the family and going against God's plans for our family.

I got myself to my feet. I felt sick and I was dizzy. I took a few minutes leaning on the back of the dinning chair to gain my composure as he continued pacing the room cursing and swearing. He walked towards the back door and opened up the sliding French doors and walked out into the garden. I assumed he had stepped out to calm himself down as I heard him take deep breaths of air into his lungs and let it out with a reasonably loud sigh. As he paced further towards the back of the garden, I picked up the keys and my handbag I saw sitting on the dining table and ran out the house and jumped in my car immediately locking my side of the door to trigger the central locking in the car. I did not look back. I had no idea if I was being followed but my spirit from when I left the house made me feel like he was around every corner. I stopped and parked up at one stage tucked in some quiet residential close. I was shaking and had to tell myself to think. 'Who can I call? Everyone will be at work? Where can I go?' My head was pounding. I looked in the rear view mirror and saw I had a golf size bump on my forehead that was burning bright red with blood trickling out from it and rolling down my face. I burst into tears. 'You're a bastard Danny! A nasty ugly bastard' is all I could muscle up. I picked up a handful of tissues and mopped up the blood. Then found some wet wipes in the in the door where my daughter always sat next to and cleaned the blood off my face and my fingers. Then I made myself a surgical wad by folding six clean tissues into a thick square and simultaneously kept placing it on my head as I drove on. I remembered one of my girlfriend's boyfriend lived in Wembley. I often looked after their child. He will help me. He did. He made me pick my daughter back up from school so that Danny wouldn't go and take her. Then we went back home to see if Danny was there and my friend convinced me to report this to the police. So I did.

Three weeks later Danny was begging and harassing me to re-book the holiday I had cancelled and had already lost over £300 I had already paid. Again he was accusing me of causing the break up of our so-called family unit. I kind of convinced myself that I would owe it to my second child when they were born not to make them grow up without their father as my eldest child had done. So I went to Jamaica. It turned out to be such a painful experience that

I vowed an oath to myself and said that 'I owed this man nothing.' That included promising to myself that, 'never again would I ever give this man a penny of my money, my time or my resources whether tangible or emotional.'

I felt beyond relieved that he missed the delivery of our baby girl. She eagerly arrived in only 1hr and 20mins from start of contraction, through to the breaking of my waters and including the delivery. She was waiting for no one. For me, his absence for such a precious moment was indeed just as precious to me.

Five weeks after the birth of our child he attacked me with a stepladder whilst our newborn baby was in my arms and for the first time, in front of my eldest child. That finally gave me the courage I needed to say and mean 'No more. This shit stops today,' and it did. Twelve years on and my second child is yet to meet her dad. He never returned and he stopped harassing me. I assume having now had his baby, he finally abandoned ship. I have always joked to myself 'that if I knew it was that easy to get rid of him, I would have had a baby for him years ago.'

During my relationship with Danny I made it through those difficult times unknowingly because of my large and close-knit family. I did not tell anyone what was happening in my home. Although, I think some of them guessed something wasn't right as my eldest daughter told me about some of the questions they had been asking her. This annoyed me, so I confronted the nosey perpetrators by telling them that I of course had no difficulty telling them what it was they wanted to know. However they needed to question me and not my child. No one ever did and I believed my boldness to challenge them threw them off the scent. However, I did need help and to this day will encourage anyone who is worried about a friend or a loved one, who is living in an abusive relationship to be sensitive in their approach but not to give up on them. Regardless of how long it takes the victim of abuse to get away from the danger or destructive relationship they find themselves in.

I was thirty-two years old when I had my second child and managed to leave this abusive relationship once and for all.

The Cross Government Definition of Domestic Violence And Abuse is:

Any incident or pattern of incidents of controlling, coercive, threatening behaviour, violence or abuse between those aged 16 or over who are or have been intimate partners or family members regardless of gender or sexuality. The abuse can encompass but is not limited to:

- *Psychological*
- *Physical*
- *Sexual*
- *Financial*
- *Emotional*

Cross-Government Definition of Domestic Violence – A Consultation Summary of Responses, Home Office, Crown Copyright December 2011, Page 19

Chapter 13: Malakh

I simply got on with life thereafter. I developed my career and accepted a managerial job within the charity for young people that I worked for. My eldest daughter was now coming up to her eighth birthday and kept asking more and more questions about her real dad and asking to meet him. That was like opening up a can of old worms for me. But this was my child and I felt the sadness she felt in her little heart for not ever having met her dad. It was hard for her because all her cousins knew and lived with both their parents. I give thanks to God for blessing me with such wonderful brothers. They never forgot either of my fatherless girls and were forever buying them their tracksuits and trainers and forever including them in the family outings. To my children and me, their uncles were more father-like figures than their father's had ever been. They were loving, consistent and involved in their lives.

Soon my eldest daughter's pinning became too much for me to bear. I bucked up the courage to make that call. 'Hello is this Trevor?'

'Hello, Trevor speaking' my heart raced and pounded when I heard his voice.

'This is your daughter's mum?' I could hear silence

Then he replied 'I had a feeling you would call' His voice was pleasant, I nearly felt the sadness slip in taking me back to the days when I had referred to this man as my finance.

'Your daughter is asking to meet you?'

'When can we meet?' he responded immediately.

Oh my goodness, I actually hadn't thought about how I would feel at actually meeting up. I think I expected the number to be wrong so I could tell my daughter I had tried and would keep trying.

'Well it's her birthday tomorrow, so what about the following weekend?'

'Yes, I'd like that' he confirmed as he sealed the arrangement.

'By the way my name is now Malakh'

When we ended the phone call, I stood there for sometime feeling nervous and praying for strength and courage.

Our daughter did so much preparation in the run up to meeting her father. She was excited, nervous and inquisitive at the same time. Over that week I noticed her need for more information about who her dad was and for an account of the life he had been leading. She began preparing twenty of her unanswered queries into a questionnaire for her dad to answer. Wow! I was truly amazed at this. I discovered a missing link in my own life and that was what I lacked to use my own acquiring skills with people I choose to have a relationship with. I had never before asked someone a string of personal questions. I grew up being told to mind our own business and that it was rude to ask people such questions so realised I had never done it.

She asked me to help but I told her that they had to be her own questions and this was the opportunity for her to ask anything that she ever wanted to know that had crossed her mind if she had the opportunity. So I left her to do it. Of course I hoped some of the questions would give me answers to my very own questions. But I also knew this was not about me.

Then the day arrived. I was nervous and had to make childcare arrangements for my eight-month-old baby whilst juggling to get my eldest ready to face the most important day in both our lives. The baby sitter rang me fifteen minutes before I was due to set off to tell me that she was running late and would get to me in about an hour's time. I pleaded with her to get to me in half that time as I had an incredible important appointment that I had to get to. I didn't want to make my daughter more nervous than she already was and get her in an upset mood too. I then had to call Trevor to let him know I was being delayed. He was accommodating but the silent and airy tone and feel I got I assumed he must have already been waiting there and the next thirty minutes to an hour were probably going to feel like it was taking forever. But there really was nothing I could do about this. It was out of my control.

When we finally got going, I was amazed at the amount of traffic on the road. This ten minute drive took us about twenty-five minutes because of two sections of road works on our journey. As I approached the restaurant we had planned to meet at I turned into the road just before the noticed a parking space on the other side of the road. That was so lucky, I thought so quickly did a three-point turn and reversed into the space. Once parked up I took another look in my rear-view mirror to glance at the car behind as I noticed a driver was sitting in his car whilst I was reversing. 'Oh my gosh' is all I could think. It was him. My heart began to thump hard and I felt so nervous. I made my daughter climb into the front seat of the car and then told her I needed to get something from the boot of the car and will be back in a second to get her.

I then opened my door and walked over to his car. Trevor's head was in the downward position and he was filling in a card. I tapped on the window and he looked up and looked as nervous as I was feeling. 'Can you give me two minutes and I'll be with you?' he asked in what almost sounded like a stutter. He was filling in some sort of a celebratory card.

'Yeah sure' I responded and went back to the car

Inside the car I looked at our daughter and her beautiful and anxious face was so ready to be put out of its misery. 'Your dad is in the car behind us' I told her.

'Really? Is he?' She looked excited and frightened, all at the same time. 'I'm scared mummy' she said as if to confirm my observations.

'I'll be with you darling so there is nothing to be scared about. You have waited a long-time for this day to happen' I said trying to comfort her.

'What's he doing? Why isn't he coming out of the car?'

'He will. He asked for two minutes because I think he was writing on something'. That answer seemed to settle her for the next thirty seconds at least.

'What's he doing now?' she asked not sure whether to turn around and look.

'I looked out the rear-view mirror and responded, 'he must still be writing because he has his head looking downwards'. As soon as I finished that sentence, his car door began to open. 'Ok, Sweet pea, he's finished and coming out the car. It's time to go'

'I'm scared'

'You'll be fine darling. Mummy is with you. I'll come around to your side of the car and get you, Ok?'

'Ok mummy' she was so very sweet is all I kept thinking. My child was also very frightened and so was I.

Trevor acknowledged me with a smile and stopped walked over to the pavement and stopped at by at the rear of my car. I walked around the bonnet of the car and kept my eye on our daughter, who kept her eye fixated on me. I opened the passenger driver's door and took hold of her hand to help her out of the car. Immediately she walked behind me and held on to my leg and peeped around my body. 'Hey Sweet pea, this is your daddy'

Trevor crouched down and lifted up his open arms to greet her. 'Hello Princess'

It took her a few seconds to move herself and then she ran over to be embraced by those awaiting arms. The meet up blew me away. I wiped away my tears quickly when I say my daughter embrace her father in that hug for the first time. He looked up at me and mimed a 'thank you.'

In the restaurant, I sat silently at the table as she asked her questions and on many occasions I had to drag back my soul that got blown away and battling with the information I already knew about him and the new information he was revealing in his answers. For all these years I thought our daughter was his first child, turns out our daughter was his second. I immediately had a flash back from when Trevor and I were engaged. He told me he

143

had had something to pay off that he and his previous girlfriend had gotten. I thought he had been referring to furniture bought on high purchase. Not a damn child.

Another question confirmed that he was now married to Elise who was the woman he had the affair with during our bridal planning. Boy did that hurt too! This was the woman who he broke up our family for. He didn't have any children with his wife whom he was married too for some six years.

A year later our daughter decided she was ready to meet her dad again for the second time. I had asked her several times if she wished to meet him again yet and each time she replied 'no, not yet mummy.' This meet up followed a series of other meet ups in restaurants and shopping centres which began opening up more cans of worms for me as I felt like I had so much unfinished business to discuss with Trevor. I was feeling angry with this man that I had once loved so much and it was stirring back up the love in my spirit. One day I decided I needed to get away because it was making me feel so low it was causing me to experience flu-like symptoms but without the flu for three weeks. I couldn't concentrate and couldn't understand why he kept coming into my dreams during the night and in my thoughts during the day. I found myself cancelling and rearranging the access visits between him and our daughter because it was becoming a painful experience to carry out. One morning I woke up and rang ahead of work and asked if I could book a week off to sort something out. That morning I packed a suitcase, walked into a bank and changed up my money into traveller cheques then walked into a travel agency and said 'I have three hundred pounds can you book me on a flight with self catering accommodation anywhere in the world leaving tomorrow please.' The travel company did. It was half term and my eldest was already with her grandmother for the holidays, so I called my mum and sister and asked if they would look after my baby from that night until I arrived back from travelling. The next morning I was on my way to Thasos in Greece for a week. It wasn't until the pilot said 'buckle up,' that I realised I had not planned this properly. I didn't even know anything about the place I was going to. I certainly had never ever travelled on a plane to anywhere in the world, totally on my own and without any of my children before. Now I was nervous.

Turns out it was the best thing I had ever done in my life. Being on your own without any distractions from anyone you could remotely know is the best time to reflect on who you are; where you're at in life; where you're going or needed to be heading; and how you plan to get there. All the problems raised its head and my mind battled for solutions and a way to cope. I went from having hot sweats when I slept to crying spells when I awoke. The first four days were the battles and the last three days brought solutions, new answers, hopes, goals and purpose. The day before leaving I had to make a very important call so went to the phone box. 'Hello Trevor I arrive back in the UK tomorrow can we meet? I'd like to discuss something with you'

'Yes what time?' he responded to accommodate my request.

'Say, seven in the evening. I'll text you when I land so that you know my plane has arrived and I will be on time'

'OK' it was as simple as that. I was convinced I needed to do this.

When we met I told him about the emotional fights I had been having with myself and that I had to tell him how angry I had been at him for the way he had treated me almost a decade ago. Up until this day, I have never forgiven him for jilting me as his pregnant fiancée and walking into the arms of another woman and for making her his wife five years later. I had never forgiven him for letting me tell him about all the abuse I was inflicted with as a child for him to turn around and cheat on me with lies of having to regularly meet with his work counsellor, who was also his trainer from the child abuse training he had done. I told him I had found out less than a year after we finished from that trainer that these child abuse review case meetings did not take place. I told Trevor that I had not forgiven him for making believe we had a future, for allowing me to fall in love him and then have him treat me as if I did not exist.

Even worse, I told him that I could not believe I was still in love with him. Trevor told me he was waiting for me to say this and he felt the exact same. The next day he walked out on Elise and their marriage. A year or so later he told me the divorce had come through and I felt less threatened thinking I had my family back together and was secure in the relationship again.

For almost two years, our family unit appeared to be back on track to where we had left off when I was pregnant with his child some ten years earlier. Then, his working patterns changed and his hours increased to meet deadlines at work, to study, attending long meetings and residential events that seemed to come up most weekends. We managed to do a couple holidays but going into our fifth year into the relationship the commitments and promises were being dragged out with excuses, problems and dilemmas that never seemed to be viable to my logical mind.

He was always gentle and sweet with me but this would many times be contradicted by the intense feeling of doubt and lack of trust I had that was growing in my mind for his growing absence away from the family home and inconsistencies to most things he would tell me that often made me think I was loosing my mind or simply got it wrong.

One of the those things was when I had to keep pestering him on behalf of his daughter to meet his mother; her grandmother whom he said he was back in contact with over the years. For about two years he kept saying she was travelling every time I asked. When we finally got to meet her I discovered more than I expected. She was not from Barbados, she was Nigerian. He told me he did not tell me this but I knew he did, plus he wore more emblems than I did to represent himself as being from Barbados when neither of his parents was from the Caribbean at all. Both were Nigerian. Even whilst we were together he had told me that he had to travel to Barbados to bury his father the year before we got together. After speaking with his mother I learnt his father died when he was a toddler. This information denied me the ability to teach our child properly about both heritages. Trevor was simply a compulsive liar. He lied about so many things. One of the biggest lies was when he had to travel abroad with his mother the year before I met her because one of his brothers had been killed in a drive-by shooting. My condolences to his mother the following year told me she had no idea what the hell I was on about and that she had not seen him in twenty years, until the month she had met me. The worse lie that brought about our ending was finding out he was still married and the birth of their son. I was devastated.

We ended six and a half years into the relationship. I was so very confused and hurting. I had put up with so much negative behaviour and was emotionally traumatised by this man who was also the father of one of my children. All this was happening during the last semester of my studies and exams for an MBA in Developing Business, whilst I was also nurturing my second year of running my own business and continuing to take care of the needs of the family. Although I kept everything ticking along, my mind became sick and I realised I desperately needed to talk to someone quickly so I made an appointment with my doctor, whom I liked. I told her all about what had happened and that I needed her to prescribe me something to help me to sleep at nights plus be able to concentrate and get me through my final exams. I shared with her the difficulties I was having trying to stop myself from crying; and how my mind kept telling me to run away and was trying to convince me not to tell anyone where I was going. She prescribed *PROZAC* (fluoxetine) for anxiety and stress. I took them for three months and it did stop those thoughts and that urging feeling to abandon my life. My doctor tried prescribing me another three months medication and informed me of the need to withdraw slowly. Against her advice, I chose not to take the prescription to a chemist as I realised I was grieving again which I identified was simply feeling bereaved from my loss. It dawned on me that something I was doing with my life was attracting these traumatic events that kept happening and playing out in my life again and again. I realised I had to face up to my internal pains, confusion, mental anguish and look at how I react to situations if I was going to heal fully.

I knew it was not going to be easy but I needed to come to terms with the abuse that I have already had inflicted in my life and remove the added self-inflictions that I managed to pour on top that stopped me from attracting my own ultimate peace and happiness. From here on in, I needed to learn to live. I needed to walk MY own talk that I had subjected hundreds if not thousands of young people, girls and women to do during my decades of working with them so that they could be encouraged and empowered to make change happen within their lives. Now this was my turn.

The partners I had encountered in my life over the years were like vampires coming to suck me dry and I had had enough of it after the abuse inflicted on me as a child. From now on, I was going to make my life and myself a happy one regardless how long it would take and declared that nobody but God was now going to change that.

I realised if I could heal myself emotionally, physically and spiritually then I would be equipped to cope, resolve, manage or even eradicate traumatic events from raising its head like it did, every few years like it was by invitation or on some conveyor belt. I realised and decided that I was worth it. This was the first breaking news I had ever declared to my own soul. I finally realised that I mattered and deserved to be loved but first I needed to love myself before expecting anyone else too.

I realised that when I loved and respected myself and was in touch with who I was and what I wanted as a vision for my life, then I would have a clearer idea about the type of people or partner I wanted to accept in to my life. I also realised for this process to be successful I needed to deal with my past and learn to forgive the people who hurt me so that I could move on and shut down some of the doors to those memories. I could no longer give my past the energy or keys to the rest of my life, my world, my future, my peace, my happiness or my wellness.

I have become peaceful with myself, which includes believing and accepting who I am now, discovering things I like and don't like and being able to feel in control. I needed to set boundaries in my life so that others and I were clear about the perimeters.

I had to change and change I did. I was forty years old when I began this journey.

Epilogue

I have spent the last six years investing in my own personal healing journey. Ironically implementing many of the same methods and tools I had spent decades imparting on to others and watching them embrace fantastic results and a purpose-led life that would leave behind their past hurts.

For many years I had felt like a prisoner trapped in the same old sad story. I was a prisoner within my thoughts that constantly replayed the hurtful memories of the past and found it far too easy to predict a future with more upsets. I would seal this in a world of secrecy yet still be able to portray the opposite to the outside world, as I fuelled myself with the opinions of others that would help me to reinforce one of the qualities I have in abundance; and that was that I was strong. Family, friends, colleagues and even clients tended to always acknowledge that I always seemed to manage well, whatever the situation. Whether coping as an independent parent on top of working full-time, with part-time studies and adding part-time work to my already heavy load, organising events and there was so many other commitments I always seemed to be juggling. So when I was in emotional or mentally pain and tried to share it, people generally responded with 'you'll be alright,' thus helping me to bleed internally instead of letting me bleed out externally.

I had learnt to keep so much of the abuse a secret after loved ones around me as a child either missed signs; plus I had been threatened as a child and then as an adult. I had internalised a great sense of personal shame and pride for the situations I had found myself in.

I had spent many years since the day I left home at aged sixteen proving to my family that I was never going to be a statistic to give society the opportunity to falsely propagate their stereotypes about black young people or a young homeless girl which predicted unemployment; pregnancy at an early age; a single parent with several fathers that did not raise their family. Although the latter itself was alien to me, even though my dad did not take up his responsibility to raise his own children with my mother. I did however come from a very large family where none of my cousins or friends lived without their fathers being in their lives daily and living in the family home.

I knew people around me over the years, generally held me in high regard. My colleagues, acquaintances, family and friends saw me as being intelligent, knowledgeable, confident, outspoken and a highly professional person. My signals for help and assistance were often even harder for anyone to have noticed because to the outside world, I knew most saw me as a self-motivated individual who was always happy, highly-spirited and an approachable woman filled with wisdom, logic and fun.

However the truth was I was my own prisoner unable to express what I really wanted in my relationships because I had not discovered the vision for my own personal happiness and needs. I had no difficulty working towards and nurturing my professional vision; a family vision; my partners' visions; a community vision; friendship visions or even generating visions in my clients whether they were young or old. But I did not seek the courage to seek one for my own personal happiness so that I could check in to see if I was on track and on the right path to nurturing and achieving the internal happiness I might want or need in my own life to enable me to keep in touch with who I am.

The fears and anxieties I experienced and carried with me in my life was another form of prison that kept me emotionally stagnated at times. I worried about being rejected yet I felt I lacked the skills or courage to confidentially reject others when their behaviour was unacceptable. I feared not being loved, though I did not feel much love for myself, which I now know was reflected in the partners I had attracted who did not sincerely and unconditionally love me for the loving and kind person that

I am. Deep down inside, I feared being disowned and abandon in all my relationships even though I did not feel happy in them.

I secretly anguished over my personal shame of being abandoned to raise my children as an independent parent rather than celebrating the wonderful job and effort I had always given and achieved, with the love and resources I had to parent. I should had been celebrating how fulfilled and blessed I felt to be a mother to two beautiful girls whom I have constantly received praises for, from both familiar faces and strangers alike whom have felt obliged to tell me my children are delightful, well mannered and absolutely lovely girls. I could also see blessings flowing into their young lives, as they are always welcomed with open arms. Yet, my heart furiously still kept bleeding internally for my own abandonment and that of my daughters' portions as they grew up not meeting their fathers till many years into their own childhood and still one of them only once.

On the other hand my fears and anxieties in the relationships were at its highest peak during confrontations with my partners and for some months after ending these negative relationships. During these times I had reached levels of emotional exhaustion for trying to smooth out the cracks and creases or coping with new crisis which were entwined in these deceitful, negative and abusive relationships that breached my trust and sent me spiraling into continuous bouts of confusion from uncovering lies and the double lives that my partners led. Then there was the ducking and diving from their unwelcome tactics whether emotionally, physically or spiritually.

Even my health would join in with the stress burdens I carried, by triggering off mouth ulcers, abscesses and serious concerns for my asthma leading to higher levels of prescribed medication. My smoking always increased during these times which has today resulted in the loss of nearly sixty percent power of my lung capacity which have kept my doctors alerting me of the dangers of me falling into the chronic obstructive pulmonary disease category if I did not stop smoking. I have now finally taken heed to their warnings and quit smoking during the completion of this book.

My exhaustion would extend to trying to hold on to my mental wellness whilst I experienced insomnia or disrupted sleep patterns which no doubt did not help my feelings of helplessness.

In my past adult relationships, I felt like a prisoner trapped in dysfunctional relationships. I made myself come to terms with the challenge of having to put up with what I thought life had thrown back at me and found myself trying to nurture normality out of the worst situations. I believed I had to work hard at salvaging the relationships even though I could see that the negatives outweighed the positives. The examples of love I experienced in some of my relationships where often based on periods of my partner's attentive nature however in reality after a spell of kindness always came spells of cunningness, vile behaviour, breach of trust or disrespect. Even though I enjoyed the spells of happiness I somehow stayed alerted waiting and watching out for what they were going to do next. The suspicion alone created the continued unhappy experiences.

I began to realise that my ever so high tolerance levels did not dictate a message of the boundary settings between my partners and I. Instead I used my tolerance to salvage the fantasies and ideas I had about families and relationships and to cover up my personal anguish and shame by continuing to work harder at making good what seemed like lost or deceitful causes.

Then one day, it dawned on me the realisation that I had to learn how to take personal responsibility for what I allow to enter or happen in my life. This did not mean I was responsible for the act of the domestic violence I found myself in, as those men are ultimately responsible for their attitude and how they choose to behave to others. However, I can take responsibility for understanding me; and the cycles I end up in. I can decide whether to respond now or in the future but I realised that what I do now will determine my future. This journey has helped me develop a positive sense of self by unfolding who I am and what values I hold in comparison to how I saw myself and what I consider my worth to be.

I have since aligned these with my personal aspirations and been able to surround myself with positive nurturing and aspiring people who make deposits in to my life instead of just taking out constant withdrawals from my emotional resources bank; spiritual resource bank; mental resource bank; and even my physical resource bank. Those latter types of people I describe as vampires whose ultimate aim is to zap, control and suck you dry because they are projecting their own insecurities on to others.

A few of the methods were not new to me as I have used them for a long time to guide me to achieving my passions in my career so that I could create myself a step by step goals to help me account for my continued professional development. However, I found when using them to focus on my emotional and spiritual health, I had to take off my own personal mask which I believe we all wear and carry around with us to help us to communicate with others in the world around us. These masks can help us guide and feed the perceptions we want others to have about us, so that we do not feel publicly exposed. I personally believe that we are all placed on this earth for a purpose and with such thinking I realised that for me to live my life to its fullest and richest potential, I needed to expose all my fears so that I could allow my soul to receive the guidance and the fullest of healing.

I have discovered how my childhood experiences and learning has shaped me in my adult life and identified those that have hindered my progression, thus requiring me to undo the learnt behaviours and mindset if I am to live a happier life. I realised many of the qualities I have found and disliked in my choice of partners were actually a deep-rooted sense of what I thought about myself. My lack of self-love and acknowledgment of my self-worth was simply being reflected back into my life to fulfill my own predictions, prophecies and my mindset.

By my ability to self-reflect and take action I have gained control; resolved many of my own personal conflicts; and identified goals to keep me moving forward with my passions for a purpose led life full of visions. I continue to use these methods still today to review and monitor my progress so that I remain in touch with who I am and to remain on track with my visions. However the most important growth I have achieved is realising that I have access to the resources I need, from within me that has made this change happen.

The other important growths that I have embraced, is the courage to reach out for help when I need it; the courage to no longer be silent; and the importance of nurturing self love which has caused me to open my heart space to tell my story in a different and empowering way with a positive look forward rather than ponder my energy on an unchangeable past.

Freeing myself from the ill effects triggered by a history of child abuse, domestic violence or any form of negative relationships is a difficult and long road to travel. It required me to take those first vital steps regardless of how uncomfortable I became or how out of my comfort zones I felt. I have discovered that this too is all part of the healing process. My aim was to first forgive myself for allowing these memories or past situations to make me sick and I looked in the mirror to affirm and tell myself that I deserved better. I then began working on my happiness in the current state and position that I found myself in and then focused on working towards the future and leaving the past alone as this could not be changed.

By working through my goals and closing the gap leading towards the visions and the dreams I have for my life has helped me to learn to take control. It needed me to hold on to hope, faith and courage as I took each step. It didn't necessarily feel easy and at times it did feel like it was an impossible and unachievable task, especially when it felt easier to struggle with my old life stories that I was familiar with, than to look at the mountains ahead of me that I needed to climb to get to the place where I could feel great about me. By breaking down the daunting goals, into smaller achievable tasks I have been able to keep moving and not become overwhelmed. The more I realised that each goal can be achieved, I then began to witness how far I had travelled to get to where I am now. The first courageous steps I took to reach out, speak out or walk out will be looked back on, as the day I discovered self love, my worth and truly began to follow the divine spirit within me.

That's not to say I or many others who are working on healing ourselves from the symptoms of post traumatic stress syndrome after having experienced crisis in our lives can eliminate our past memories but what I do now know is I chose not to be limited by the feelings of unworthiness and fear from my past experiences. I no longer tell the story or react to the story in the same way and I now refuse to attract anything into my life that I perceive as being a negative hindrance or threat to my personal happiness or to this beautiful soul of mine.

I have conquered the depths of suicidal-depression and worked through the feelings associated with loneliness, abandonment, anger and lack of self-love. These are itself great achievements which could be judged by my ability to now talk openly about them without personally experiencing distress signals of living through such pain and shame, day in and day out as it once used to create in my life. I now accept I have a responsibility for feeding my soul with positive elements so that it can heal, grow, live, celebrate and vibrantly prosper in the time that this body I possess remains for me on this earth. I now embrace that I have a responsibility to ensure the decisions I take regarding my life or the situations I find myself in, leaves me feeling perfectly ok and assured that it is in the best interest for my spirit and my life too.

Becoming responsible for the decisions I make about me and my life becomes even more important when making a decision to enter into an intimate relationship and stay in one. If I feel there is not a compatible and spiritual fit, I am now more determined and confident in promptly ending that relationship instead of being over tolerant and bruising my emotional well being along the way. Better still I've learnt to avoid walking straight into and staying in any form of relationships without feeling great about me and who surrounds me.

To develop my awareness about relationships I have given myself permission to date without commitment. Something I had never done before. I now give myself permission to ask, request, seek out, test or even observe to make sure I feel assured about our compatibility and communication skills. My standards have risen and so has my boundaries and lack of tolerance.

Amazingly, other strategies like prayer, meditation, and forgiveness have taken care of all associated anger I had to those in my past so I know I do not now judge my standards as being a form of hang ups I have carried from my past.

My strategy for remaining at peace and happy within myself is not to give up love of self; self control; nurturing of my spirit or working towards the visions I now have for my life. Therefore responding and ending negative behaviour within a relationship begins by clearly stating these from the initial beginning of any relationship and ensuring my choices, decisions and reactions positively supports this. This does not mean I presume or look out for downfalls in others however I have discovered the importance of not accepting intimate relationships into my world based on face value.

By focusing my attention on building up friendships alongside practice or long periods of sexual abstinence with partners has provided the added ability and space to exercise clearer thinking, judgment and selective assessment of other people's character, qualities and intentions which will always evolve over time and especially during what is always referred to as the honeymoon period of any intimate relationship. These are therefore not always so obvious or known on the first few times, weeks or even months of meeting someone. This space also allows me to be in-tuned with the spirit that lies within others and myself. But most importantly has been vital in making sure I am feeling confident and assured within my own spirit and that decisions I take remain in the best interest for feeding my internal spirit for positive growth.

In the case of one of my partners whose violence escalated from verbal to physical attacks during pregnancy, I have to admit to myself that there were so many other signs and symptoms he displayed that indicated his need to exercise control over me prior to his switch in reactions. Before this, my spirit had already been awoken to fears and doubts by his negative reactions, behaviour, attitude, temperament to what I felt were normally simplistic matters and his attempts to add confusion into my world alongside my own self doubts which were triggered within only three months after meeting this man; having slept with him and having him take up residency within my home and refusing to leave or end the relationship. It occurred to me that when I buy groceries for my family I do so by first applying some basic principals like what meals am I planning; check if I've got or found the correct ingredients I need; carry out quality checks to see if the produces are fit for consumption of our choice, as my children refuse to eat fruit or vegetables which have a single bruise or mark on it, however much I try to persuade them that the dark bits on bananas consist of more vitamins. However, I am regiment at checking the dates, origin of products and even the ethics behind certain food trades because of personal preferences. For certain menus I would need to know if the produce are grown seasonally and can be purchased locally and if it's not I might need to go for the backup frozen ingredients. If a produce is more costly than I would happily pay for it, I'd have to calculate the possibilities of replacing that ingredient with an alternative one or simply decide if that particular dish was more hassle than it's worth based on cooking method, cooking time, taste buds, etc. and decide whether to abandon the menu altogether. There are many times I have come across produce that I have tried and didn't quite like them and know with certainty that I would not try it again, spend my money on it or allocate time preparing a dish on one of my family menus. There are also certainly some aisles that I don't even walk down because my food choices or the health or personal needs of mine, my children or my household is not catered for down those aisles. So would find it easy to walk past. However the fact remains that before or the minute I walk into a shop, I have already begun the thinking, planning and calculating process of making decisions based on the relationship we have with food. This process continues once it's introduced into the household and again at periodic times because preferences change and so does the relationship with that dish on the menu.

I realised I had never once worked through or considered what my own preferences or choices were for selecting a relationship that I had decided to be intimate with. At the age of forty I began to learn who I was spiritually and regulate the type of relationships I wanted around me. It became vitally important to be in control and be proactive in reducing any possibility of becoming gullible, manipulated or duped by negative, insecure and dysfunctional people again at the detriment of my spiritual growth.

I've learnt to open my heart space to both my faith and my own spirituality by learning how to apply prayer or meditation into my life to find peace, resolve, solutions, passion, hope and guidance to address issues that affect my life. I'm becoming more in-tuned and steered by my own spirituality and free will in recognising if choices I have taken are best for me. If they are not, my spiritual consciousness alerts me to trust my gut feelings and to voice my needs or change the situation until I feel spiritually in tuned with God's purpose for my life. At different stages of my journey I've noticed how more courageous, focused and determined I have become as I grow and feed my spiritual life alongside some of my religious practices. I consciously proportion time aside to attend motivational or self development workshops, listen to inspirational audio studies, attend retreats or play music that will contribute to uplifting my spirit, my morale and create a tranquil environment around me.

Making change happen in your life will mean you will have to take those scary steps to be able to heal yourself. It's going to be necessary to reflect on all aspects of your life to see and locate where you are at now in your life and where you would like to be or need to be. The gap presented in between the two points of your life, needs to be accompanied with achievable and reachable goals that helps you to move forward and move you nearer to your ultimate dream. By building up aspects of your life whether it's your relationships with others, education, social life, family, finance, home life, career, business, support networks, spiritual life, diet, health, nutrition, wellness, exercise, stress, play, hobbies, free-time, fun, self esteem, environment and life's purpose in your own life, will enable you to make the decisions you believe are suitable and comfortable for you and your life; at that time of your life whilst looking into the future.

By making yourself feel stronger you will be able to apply and rely on your better judgments and life choices. You can begin to avoid or manage your emotional lows or feel more equipped to moving yourself around them and in to a better place. With your new ability to self-care for you and your needs, you will develop the ability to tell your story in a new and uplifting way that does not cause you to feel like the world is crashing down around you.

The best thing I've found since reviewing where I once was and where I am now in my life, is knowing that I am clearer in my thinking and I'm on track to achieving the desires and visions I have; and have even added new ones along the way. I am conscious about how I utilise my time and whom I spend it with. This isn't to say I don't find myself juggling my time and energy to help others, of course I do. After all I am a mother, a sister, an aunty, a daughter, a friend, a neighbour, a church member, a business owner, an entrepreneur, a presenter, a speaker, an author etc etc etc. However, the difference is I am no longer putting my own needs last or giving out open door invitations for such negative forces to walk right into my life that doesn't acknowledge the person I am or celebrate my worth as joyfully as I celebrate others or my friends and family celebrate mine.

Over the years I have personally used coaching, mentoring and other support services too; and have delivered such support programmes for individuals as they worked towards overcoming particular obstacles and fears they faced in their lives. It's been a great way of learning new skills or knowledge by engaging in goal-focused; client-proactive; and professional-accountability relationships to face my challenges and focus on solutions by shifting the mindset to achieve them. Through these types of supportive relationships you can further learn to tap your internal resources that we are actually all equipped with to generate solutions and healing outcomes that suit our own lives.

You can obtain further information and support on self-healing from my website:

www.malakhzebulun.com

Bibliography:

Protecting children from sexual abuse: A guide for parents and carers, NSPCC 2008

http://www.barnardos.org.uk/what_we_do/our_projects/sexual_abuse.htm

Debra Allnock (2010) Children and young people disclosing sexual abuse: An introduction to the research, NSPCC, London

Chaplin, Rupert, Faltley, John and Smith, Kevin (eds.) (2011) Table 2.04. In: Crime in England and Wales 2010/11: findings from the British Crime Survey and police recorded crime (PDF). London: National Statistics. p.43.

Elizabeth Lovell (2002), Children and young people who display sexually harmful behaviour, NSPCC, London

Chaplin, Rupert, Faltley, John and Smith, Kevin (eds.) (2011) Table 2.04. In: Crime in England and Wales 2010/11: findings from the British Crime Survey and police recorded crime (PDF). London: National Statistics. p.62

Depression Fact Sheet, (2012), Rethink Mental Illness 2011, London

The World Health Report 2001, Mental Health: New Understanding, New Hope Geneva: World Health Organisation p10, (2001)

Spataro J et al, Impact Of Child Sexual Abuse On Mental Health, British Journal Of Psychiatry 184 pp416-21, (2004)

Facts & Figures, Frequently Asked Questions, National Treatments Agency for Substance Misuse, NHS, London, www.nta.nhs.uk/facts-faqs.aspx

Crisis Research briefing: Young, hidden and homeless (April 2012), CRESR for The hidden truth about homelessness, PDF pg1.

The Holy Bible, Leviticus 18:6, New International Version, 1984

Kelly Mattison, Speaking Out acclaim for survivors of childhood abuse, The Guardian Newspaper, Wednesday 25 November 2009

The Penguin Dictionary of Psychology, Second Edition, Arthur S. Reber, Penguin Books, 1985, 1995, London, Page 439

Understanding mental health problems,
http://www.mind.org.uk/assets/0001/7308/Understanding _mental_health_problems_2011.pdf

Women's Aid, Domestic Violence: Frequently Asked Questions Factsheet 2009

Cross-Government Definition of Domestic Violence – A Consultation Summary of Responses, Home Office, Crown Copyright December 2011, Page 19

Further Reading

I want to introduce you to my friend Joseph Seiler, an author. I believe sometimes when you look at other peoples lives you realise yours isn't so bad. I also realise how much our lives are so interconnected to God's and the answers to our own journey will always be revealed if we stop to tune in

Up From Paralysis is about having a more successful life, whether that be success in career/business or success in personal life. Success in life is rooted in happiness. Joseph has shared his journey of discovery of 'how it all works' for him, when it comes to listening to that tiny whisper of wisdom some call intuition, Spirit, Guidance. When we connect with the wisdom and ease of that 'other side,' which is actually 'inside,' we are more successful in everything that we interact with. Joseph experienced the disease Guillain-Barre Syndrome (GBS) which paralyzed him very quickly. He then slowly healed. In the paralysis state, his mind was at a heightened level of awareness. Unable to do anything physical, he applied himself to understanding the vivid messages that became so present from the 'other side.' He provides a chronicle of the GBS, but more, he provides a detailed account of the discoveries made available to him, explained in his own simple language. Learn how to, through increased clarity, live a more successful life in all dimensions.

Joseph Seiler MCC
www.yournaturaledge.com

SELF HELP SERVICES:

MALAKH ZEBULUN OFFICIAL:

Malakh Zebulun is a Change Agent for Empowered Lives; working with women who are ready to embrace breaking negative and hurtful cycles that keep repeating in their lives. Malakh has 30 years of experience working with vulnerably adults in crisis situations and is NLP certified. Further qualifications include MBA, and as a Trainer, Manager and Community and Youth Worker

Her signatory workshops are from her series of 'Learning To Let Go' for women.

Visit Malakh Zebulun's website for information on workshops, coaching and support services, self-empowerment resources and to request her for speaking engagements.

Website: www.malakhzebulun.com
Email: pr@malakhzebulun.co.uk

TRAINING EDUCATORS C.I.C.:

Malakh Zebulun is one of the co-Founders and Directors at Training Educators C.I.C. which exists solely to provide support for children and young adults who have been the victims of abuse, or who are at risk of being exposed to abuse, albeit directly or indirectly.

They're trained and experienced team, work closely with schools and other bodies that care for children, to educate this vulnerable group about safer relationships, self-esteem, empowerment and so much more.

Their programs are designed with specific outcomes that will equip the next generation with the necessary social skills to positively engage and contribute within society.

Website: www.trainingeducators.co.uk
Email: info@trainingeducators.co.uk

DIVERSITYINCARE:

The effects of past and current abuse have lead many women to a life filled with drugs and alcohol mis-use to block out their reality, emotional pain and memories.

DiversityInCare's mission is to prevent and reduce drug and alcohol related issues for individuals living in disadvantaged communities throughout the UK. They will develop specialist services that provide continuous support and transform how care is delivered.

Website: www.diversityincare.org.uk
Email: info@diversityincare.org

Printed in Great Britain
by Amazon.co.uk, Ltd.,
Marston Gate.